WALKS FOR ALL AGES
THE BLACK COUNTRY

WALKS *FOR* ALL **AGES**

THE BLACK COUNTRY

BRENDAN HAWTHORNE

BRADWELL
BOOKS

Published by Bradwell Books
9 Orgreave Close Sheffield S13 9NP
Email: books@bradwellbooks.co.uk

British Library Cataloguing in Publication Data: a catalogue record for this book is available from the British Library.

1st Edition

ISBN: 9781909914377

Print: CPI Group (UK) Ltd, Croydon, CR0 4YY

Design by: Erik Siewko Creative, Derbyshire.
eriksiewko@gmail.com

Photograph Credits: © Brendan Hawthorne
and credited seperately where applicable.

Maps: Contain Ordnance Survey data
© Crown copyright and database right 2014

Ordnance Survey licence number 100039353

The information in this book has been produced in good faith and is intended as a general guide. Bradwell Books and its authors have made all reasonable efforts to ensure that the details are correct at the time of publication. Bradwell Books and the author cannot accept any responsibility for any changes that have taken place subsequent to the book being published. It is the responsibility of individuals undertaking any of the walks listed in this publication to exercise due care and consideration for the health and wellbeing of each other in the party. Particular care should be taken if you are inexperienced. The walks in this book are not especially strenuous but individuals taking part should ensure they are fit and able to complete the walk before setting off.

INTRODUCTION

IN PUTTING TOGETHER THIS BOOK OF WALKS IN AND AROUND THE BLACK COUNTRY I HAVE SEEN SOME OF THE MOST BEAUTIFUL SECTIONS OF COUNTRYSIDE THAT I BELIEVE THIS COUNTRY HAS TO OFFER.

As a born and bred Black Countryman I have grown up with the canal network that criss-crosses our region, harking back to when the industrialised waterways were the safest and fastest mode of transport from the late 18th through to the mid-20th century, when road and rail offered far better alternatives. By the time I was growing up in the 1960s very few boats were still carrying freight along these waterways, which were falling into disrepair and decline. The waterways are now going through a renaissance as part of the leisure industry and many voluntary groups have been set up to maintain and preserve the canal heritage that you see today.

On many of these walks I have seen nature reclaim its hold on the post-industrial landscapes that exist throughout this region and turn man-made structures into glorious features which we can enjoy today.

Many of the walks are along canals and disused railway lines or around the remnants of mining and manufacturing industries. I have met many helpful and friendly people on these walks and have chatted and found out a little more about the locale from their interesting and intriguing stories. It is, however, not advisable to walk these routes alone. Apart from the usual health and safety issues these walks can take you through both urbanised and very remote areas so please be aware of personal safety at all times.

A big thank you goes to Mick, who helped me find the start point to my walk around Cannock Chase, and to my old mate Den, who took me around some of his old haunts with a few tales to tell!

I hope you enjoy your adventures in this book as much as I have. Best foot forward!

WREN'S NEST

IF YOU'RE INTERESTED IN WILD PLANTS, BIRDS AND BATS,
AS WELL AS CAVES, CASTLES, INDUSTRIAL LIME PITS, OH,
AND MILLIONS OF YEARS OF FOSSILISED GEOLOGY, LOOK NO
FURTHER THAN THE WREN'S NEST, DUDLEY!

Imagine if you will for a moment, warm tropical seas gently rippling on brilliant white beaches, Dudley Bugs (trilobites) scuttling around in the shallows behind the breakwaters as ferns and trees gently sway on newly wooded fringes. Down in the slightly deeper waters shellfish feed as sea snails and corals live off gentle currents.

Unfortunately, travelling to Dudley will only get you halfway to this paradise. The other is to be able to travel back in time over 400 million years!

Set in the heart of the industrial Black Country the Wren's Nest outcrop of rock is one of several hills formed by glaciers as they were forged from new landscapes on their migration south during the last Ice Age. A short drive from Dudley, Sedgely or Tipton town centres the Wren's Nest Nature Reserve incorporates Wren's Nest Hill and Mons Hill.

The site is of international importance and provides natural and man-made habitat for wild birds, bats and flowers as well as several species of broad-leafed trees. The Birmingham Canal and Dudley Canal Tunnel runs a little way in the distance though a canal arm that was connected to the lime workings under what is now the Seven Sisters Cave network.

Limestone was an important rock commercially for the region. It was used locally as stone for building, for furnaces in iron production as well as being processed for plaster, metal flux for braising and soldering purposes and also to neutralise the acidity levels in soil on farmland as lime is alkaline by nature.

This short walk can be extended if required by using site maps; however, it is strenuous in parts. Stout walking boots are necessary as paths can be muddy, have loose shale and can be rocky.

The route will take you through woods and on to old quarry rock faces. You are advised not to climb and to respect any safety signs and fences, keeping to designated paths at all times. If you are a fossil collector or have an interest in this field of geology please do not use hammers or remove fossils from the rocky outcrops. You can pick up a few small specimens from the loose material on the ground.

THE WALK

1.   Off Wren's Hill Road follow signs to Wren's Nest Nature Reserve and park on car park. There may be weekend parking restrictions, please check. Local information is available from the site managers office. With your back to the car park turn left and walk down the slight hill on the roadside until you see the entrance gate to the reserve. This is adjacent to 'The Caves' public house.

2.   Follow the path round a right-hand bend and past a meadow on your right. You will now see the geology laid

THE BASICS

Distance: 3 miles / 5km
Gradient: Steep and slippery in places
Severity: Moderate walk
Time: 1¼ hrs
Stiles: One
Map: OS Explorer 219 (Wolverhampton & Dudley)
Path description: Variable – rocky, gravel and earth
Start point: Wren's Nest car park. (GR SO 935922)
Parking: Local car park and is close to bus routes. (DY1 3SB)
Dogs: Allowed but site rules need to be adhered to
Toilets: None
Refreshments: None

down in the Silurian age. Slightly to your left there is a clearing with outcrops of rock and on your right you will see an outcrop of limestone with rock strata falling diagonally from left to right. This feature is known as the ripple beds formed in shallow seas from millions of tiny and shell-like sea creatures. The hillock on the left is from deeper waters and is known as the reef mound. As you walk past the outcrops you may be lucky enough to see orchids in bloom, usually in June.

3. Ascend the steps to reach a viewing area overlooking the ripple beds and the reef mound before rejoining the path. Walk up through the trees turning right at the 'bat' marker. On your right you will see the 'Seven Sisters' caves. The top section of caverns is known as the light caves. When the limestone was mined here light flooded into the shafts and helped mineworkers to recognise the rich seams. When mining went to second and third levels, extracting rock became difficult so a canal branch was constructed.

4. Follow the path past the old farm site on your left. You will see a ring of trees that mark the site and on to Murchison's View where you can see Dudley Castle ahead and Clent Hills to your right. Turner's Hill is situated to the left of the castle and is made of dolerite that was used to stabilise the caves. Between Clent Hills and the Castle you can see Dudley's Top Church and the town centre, which are built on Carboniferous coal measures.

5. Continue down and along the 99 steps (there aren't!) and turn right at the bottom, continuing on the main path until you reach a marker post where you will turn left. You will pass the curious 'red limestone' on your left. Continue through an open wooded area and down another set of steps known as Rob's Steps. On your right you will have a meadow and views of Dudley Castle. On your right you will see a small path that takes you into Bluebell Wood. You may take a slight detour here and rejoin the main path a little further along.

6. Continue along the path and turn left on path through Roots Valley. Notice the cliff faces through the open tree canopies, then take further steps down and turn right.

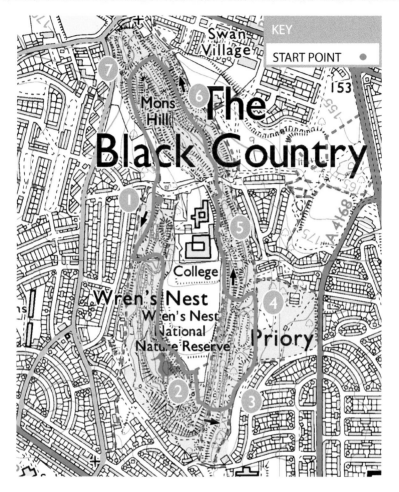

Here you can turn left to the car park or continue right. Turn left and cross the road, continue following the path and turn left. Continue through a stile and keep left to reach the Mons Hill area of the site.

7. Continue via various flights of steps until you reach a butterfly marker and then turn left before climbing more steps! Look to the pool on your right. Turn left and again ascend more steps, turning left onto a broad path that was once used to drive cattle along from Dudley to Sedgley. Continue along the main path until you reach the road and car park

SMESTOW VALLEY

SMESTOW VALLEY IS KNOWN FOR ITS WILDLIFE AND COVERS AN AREA OF AROUND 120 ACRES CONSISTING OF MEADOWS, SCRUBLAND AND WOODLAND. THE RESERVE IS IN CLOSE PROXIMITY TO SMESTOW BROOK AND THE STAFFORDSHIRE TO WORCESTERSHIRE CANAL.

There is pedestrian access to the reserve twenty-four hours per day. Car park access is available from 7.30am and, depending upon the time of year, until 5pm to 11pm variable.

Much of the reserve is under the canopy of many broad-leaved trees suggesting the antiquity of the area. This cover affords welcome shade in hot sun and can give a little shelter when the weather is more inclement. The old railway station is still very much in evidence and also the goods warehouse which you will find opposite the station at the far end of the car park.

The walk follows the path of an old railway track, now removed, and links up with the canal network through examples of breathtaking urban countryside. There are opportunities here for photographers to capture images of unusual plant specimens, wildlife and canal life! There are opportunities for a family walking day out serviced with well-maintained paths and picnic areas for walkers and cyclists alike.

The paths for much of the walk are gravelled and broad. There is some disabled access to parts of the reserve. This is very much dog-walking territory and, as I found when walking this route, the locals are very friendly and will stop for a quick chat! There are also areas of this walk, though, when you will not see another person for quite some time. If you just want to hear birdsong and distant rippling waters then this is the place for you. Be aware that some areas can be a little boggy after heavy rain and that these areas remain wet for some time after a storm. Good stout shoes or decent walking boots are recommended. Whilst en route, look out for the wild garlic that grows along the banks and ditches of various sections of the walk. It should be obvious when the pungent odour in early to mid-June gives it away!

When joining the canal section of the walk please be aware of the mooring points along canal towpaths and please respect the privacy of people on their boats, either residential or tourist. Many will strike up a short conversation and wave as they move slowly along the waterways at a similar speed to walking pace.

THE BASICS

Distance: 4 miles / 6.5km
Gradient: some inclines
Severity: easy
Time: 1¾ hrs
Stiles: One
Map: OS Explorer 219 (Wolverhampton & Dudley)
Path description: Variable: tarmac, gravel and earth
Start point: Old station building, Smestow Valley. (GR SO 891999)
Parking: Local car park and is close to bus routes. (WV6 8NX)
Toilets: At tea room (customers only)
Dogs: Allowed but site rules need to be adhered to
Refreshments: Tea room

SMESTOW VALLEY WALK

1. To the left-hand side of the old station building look for the information boards that take you to the 'platform' side of the station. Upon reaching a gate with wheelchair access continue through this gate and along a gravel path. Ignore the gate on your left but continue along the old railway track towards Compton.

2. At a fingerpost that states 'Compton ½ mile' continue straight ahead at a gated section where there is a small bridge. Cross the bridge over a brook and then turn right along main path. Continue over girder-work bridge. Turn right at next junction in path and walk towards the metal gates with the words 'Wolverhampton Environment Centre' set into them. Cross the narrow

    road and then continue left and through the trees turning right onto a broad path. Turn right and walk downhill. There is an opportunity to see a beautiful stretch of meadows on the right. This section can be boggy in damp weather

3. Walk up to the canal locks. Continue across the bridge and turn left onto the canal towpath. You are now heading towards Wightwick. At the next sequence of locks ahead you will see a bridge. The locks will be marked Wightwick Locks. Turn right at the gate and up an incline to the bridge and onto the crossroads at Wightwick. Over the road you will see The Mermaid public house. Turning left along the Bridgnorth Road will lead to the entrance to Wightwick Manor should you wish to visit. Admission charges are in force here unless you are a member of The National Trust. There is a grounds and house or grounds only ticket that will need to be paid for at the visitor reception centre on site.

4. Rejoin the canal at the last exit and turn left, walking back along the towpath to retrace your steps for a short while. Continue along the towpath and walk past the number 58 bridge. To your left you will see a small overflow. To your right you will see the covered path of Smestow Nature Reserve. Be aware of boat moorings and ahead of you will be a bridge that gives access to the 'Oddfellows' public house.

5. Continue along to Compton 59 bridge. Walk under the bridge where more locks come into view at Compton number 60 bridge. This is a great place to rest and take

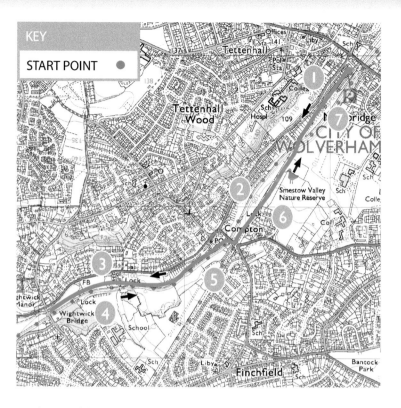

in some of the scenery. There are information boards and a small picnic site also situated here. At this bridge turn right and rejoin the Smestow Valley walk. Continue along the path to a gate. Turn left onto the main path; you will see some houses here. Turn immediate left and onto a 'higher' level path through a narrow stile gate. Turn right to walk towards the old station.

6. Cross the girder-work bridge and walk past the waymarker. There are views of the canal here. At the small bridge on your left-hand side go through the gate on the right-hand side to join the canal towpath. A red brick bridge will come into view at this point. On the right you will see modern houses with a magnificent willow overhanging the water. Beware of boat moorings.

7. Before reaching the next bridge turn left through a gate and left again to another gate opposite a white house. Turn right on a path to a fingerpost outside the station. This is the car park and start point. If you wish to extend your walk towards Aldersley do so along the path past the rangers' red brick building on the left.

SALTWELLS NATURE RESERVE

SALTWELLS NATURE RESERVE IS SAID TO BE THE LARGEST OF ITS KIND IN THE WEST MIDLANDS AND INCORPORATES SALTWELLS WOOD, WHICH IS SITUATED CENTRALLY TO THE 247-ACRE SITE.

The name of Saltwells derives from the brine spas that rose up as a result of early mine workings. This phenomenon in turn gave rise to the area being advertised as 'the place to go for the healing qualities of its medicinal spring waters' in the 19th century.

The reserve is situated off Saltwells Road where you will find a turning for Saltwells Lane. Follow the nature reserve signage past a 'no through road' traffic sign. Continue to the car park; it will be in front of you and there you will find an information board. To the left of the car park gate you will see another lane at the end of which you will find The Saltwells Inn, which is a lovely family pub which serves fine bar meals all day.

The site of 'Saltwells' once formed part of Lord Dudley's estate after Pensnett Chase was enclosed in 1785. The wood provided charcoal for the birth of the industrialised iron industry. There is an abundance of wildlife here including bluebells and wild garlic as well as wild flowers, insects and birdlife.

There are early remnants of earthworks on this site, and evidence of mine working going back to the 14th century still survives today. Primarily iron ore and coal would be extracted here from shallow seams, and then deeper workings ensued through the use of Roman-style bell pits.

Saltwells Colliery, which consisted of over thirty pits, was served in 1851 by the Pensnett railway system linking the towns of Brierley Hill and Cradley. You can still see where the railway track ran through the site if you look very closely!

Doulton's Claypit (previously called Saltwells Clay Field) provided fine clay for sanitary wares and china for 70 years until its demise in the 1930s. Nature has now reclaimed its rights on the landscape and it is now home to rare birds, beautiful orchids and common lizards, snakes and newts This scarred landscape offers an exciting view of rock strata laid down over 300 million years ago. To the south of the wood lies Mushroom Green, the hamlet once known for its chain making in the 19th century. You will see a reed swamp there now which is a haven for wildlife.

THE BASICS

Distance: 4 miles / 6.5km
Gradient: Some inclines
Severity: Moderate walk
Time: 1¾ hrs
Stiles: Three
Map: OS Explorer 219 (Wolverhampton & Dudley)
Path description: Variable: gravel and earth
Start point: Saltwells Nature Reserve car park. Grid ref: SO 933868
Parking: Local car park and is close to bus routes. Postcode: DY5 1AX
Toilets: At Saltwells Inn
Dogs: Allowed but site rules need to be adhered to
Refreshments: At Saltwells Inn

SALTWELLS N.R. WALK

1. To the rear of the car park follow signs for the 'Murray Grey Trail'. The gate you need has a white top rail. Continue along a broad path past the Pensnett railway memorial sculpture. At the waymarker turn right and up through a flight of a few steps leading to woodland. There is a small bench on the right-hand side. Continue up a steady incline to a waymarker on the right-hand side.

2. At the gatepost turn left and at a short break in an ivy-covered hedge turn right and pick up waymarkers. There is an information board on your left detailing the bell pits. Continue on the gravel path up a slight incline and follow the route to the right. Follow the path to the right and then the waymarker to the left across a grassed area. Continue to a T-junction. Turn left following the marker on your right. Within a few yards continue to a main road by walking through one gate and then a roadside gate. To your right across the road you will see another gate to continue the walk. Take care crossing the road here.

3. Follow the path to a sharp right turn over a concreted section of path to gain views of clay pits on your left. Follow the waymarker across a bricked area and at the crossroads in the path go straight on to an information board describing the coalfields. Here the path crosses the canal.

4. Continue over a planked bridge and through a metal gate to a waymarker and turn left. On the main path head for metal gates and go through both gates crossing a small track. Avoid the gate directly in line with you, and head for the gate to the right with a nature reserve sign.

5. Walk across defined paths in grassland towards a gate opposite going through the narrow stile gate before reaching the main gate. Continue across the next field to another wooden stile-type gate opposite. Take a narrow path to a flight of railway sleeper steps keeping the wire mesh fence on your left. Descend to a small flight of railway sleeper steps and then turn left. On your left is a pool with irises. Follow the path to right. There is a gated field adjacent to the main road. Retrace your steps back along the path and take the left fork of a 'V' in the main path and then follow the central pathway towards a small clump of trees. Walk back through the series of stiles and metal gates crossing fields back towards the canal. Turn right over the canal crossing.

6. Turn right at a waymarker to view the bridge and canalside. Turn back onto the reserve path, turning left, where you will see an iron canal bridge at the junction. Return to the main path, following it round to the right. Continue through the gate, crossing the road safely, towards another gate slightly to your right.

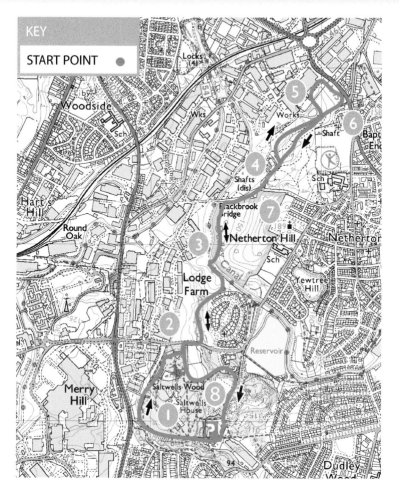

7. Turn left on the main route to a fingerpost with carved butterflies. Turn left at the junction and follow the Doulton Trail markers to the left and immediately turn right after the marker towards a flight of steps. Turn left at the top and follow the trail to the left following a waymarker, then turn right at the main junction. There are brick-built walls here. Turn left to an information board and Doulton's Claypit.

8. Continue past the information board and rejoin the main path. Turn left and walk towards a metal gate with a white top rail and on to the car park.

WIGHTWICK

This well-defined walk of mainly flat paths with some steady inclines takes in the timeless beauty of a naturalised canal system popular with leisure boats and along the route of the Smestow railway where the tracks are now removed to provide safe pathways and cycle routes.

The walk will take us along the Staffordshire and Worcester canal where rail, road and canal as well as the Smestow Brook run vaguely parallel to the main arterial Bridgnorth Road.

The Mermaid public house will be our start point here. Local on-road parking is available a short distance away, or speak to the management at the pub if you are intending to dine there.

The walk takes us along an old canal route, engineered by James Brindley. Generally the older a canal is the more bends and lock gates it will contain. This was due to the builders going around natural contours in the land. Later Thomas Telford's canals tended to go through, over or under natural features. A personal maxim reflecting this is 'Brindley's Bends and Telford's Tunnels'!

Along the towpaths look out for insect life as well as hedgerow habitats and some small wildlife. In summer there is an array of airborne nymphs and butterflies. You may be lucky and see birds of prey overhead and we haven't even started to talk about the vast array of boats, gardens and, of course, the very interesting people you meet along the way. As ever with any canal towpath please be aware of the mooring posts. These can be tripping hazards but form an important part of canal life. They are usually white capped and concentrated around lock gates to moor boats queuing at the locks during busy periods.

Life on the margins of rail and canal are interesting. You will see the cultivated gardens of private properties leading down to the wild rushes of the canal. On the return part of the journey you will access the Smestow rail route via a narrow lane that will take you through the Smestow Nature Reserve and back to the canal junction with The Mermaid pub.

Along this section of the main road you will see the Wightwick Manor Estate, now owned by The National Trust. The manor can be accessed a little way along the Bridgnorth Road in the direction of Bridgnorth. There is a tea room there, though entrance fees are charged to enter the grounds unless you are a member of the National Trust.

THE BASICS

Distance: 6 miles / 10.5km
Gradient: some steep inclines
Severity: Moderate walk
Time: 2¾ hrs
Stiles: None
Map: OS Explorer 219 (Wolverhampton & Dudley)
Path description: Variable: gravel and earth
Start point: Mermaid Inn, Wightwick. (GR SO 867983)
Parking: On street near Mermaid Inn. (WV6 8BN)
Toilets: Nearest at Mermaid Inn
Dogs: Allowed but site rules need to be adhered to
Refreshments: Mermaid Inn

WIGHTWICK WALK

1. Opposite The Mermaid Inn access the canal off Windmill Lane. Turn right along the towpath in the direction of Bridgnorth and walk under the road bridge. Here you will find an information board.

2. As you continue along the towpath heading towards Castlecroft Bridge number 55, here you will see cultivated gardens giving way to nature. There are rushes and mature trees on a left-hand bend and if look around you may find nodules of 'shiny glassy metal'. This is a by-product of the steel industry and is commonly known as 'slag' or 'klinker'. Walk towards the blue brick Mopps Farm Bridge, numbered 54. To the left on a raised section of land lie Pools Hall cottages. Enjoy the natural beauty!

3. Continuing along the path on your left you will have Langlade Farm and on your right is Twin Oaks farm where the pools are situated. Look at the hedgerows of wild roses as you follow the path to the left. There is a gap in the hedgerow where you will get good views of the pools. Further on is Dibbingsdale Bridge, which carries a small road across it. The bridge has a pipeline in front of it. On the left is a boat dock. Continue along the towpath following a bend to the left to a sequence of lock gates known as Dibbingsdale Locks. Cross the towpath to the other side of the canal; there is no choice! Look to the left to see the water system feeding and draining the locks. On the embankment to your right there is a vast array of poppies that open in June.

4. Follow a right-hand bend to another flight of locks named Ebbstree Locks, then continue to a sharp left turn on the towpath where there are moorings and gardens on your right. There is a whole micro system here! Continue to Awbridge Locks and number 49 bridge there will be an old coal wharf on your right. Leave the canal, turning left, and follow a small lane uphill named Union Lane. Turn slightly right along Flash Lane, known for flooding under the bridge! Take a small steep pathway to your right before the railway bridge and then cross the bridge to join the Smestow Railway Walk, joining the gravel path via a gate.

5. Follow the main path where there are plenty of opportunities to stop and rest with picnic tables and benches along the route. This is a steady incline through beautiful English countryside. Cross the small girder-work bridge over a road and stay on main path.

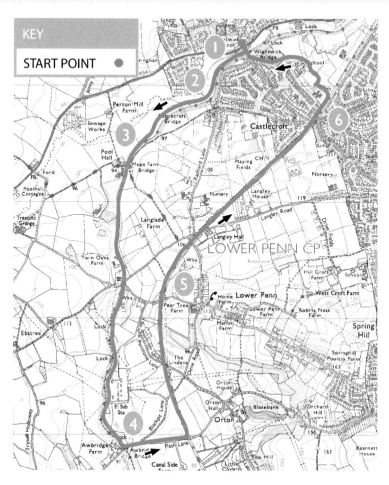

6. Remain on the main path for a considerable time heading towards Castlecroft. Stay
    on the main path over a sequence of bridges. Eventually you will reach a sign post on
    the left stating Castlecroft Railway Walk. At road level there are shops here that are
    accessed up a flight of steps to your right. Continue the walk under the road bridge.
    Pass the school on your left and take the next left turning that leads you through
    meadowland and fields. Keep left on the path and do not go straight on at an electrical
    box. Stay on the sandy path. There will be a large building on your left. Walk through a
    single gatepost staying on the defined path. In front of you you will see Wightwick Lock
    after passing some playing fields on your left. Cross the lock section turning left on the
    towpath towards Wightwick Bridge. Take the small path to the right at Windmill Lane
    bridge to access the main road via a gate and return to the start point.

SHEEPWASH NATURE RESERVE

The reserve is accessible from Tame Road where there is plenty of on-street parking available. Look out for the Tame Bridge public house, formerly The Seven Stars, which will serve as a landmark for the start point.

Food is served here from midday until three and on cooler days the pub is host to a 'proper' open fire in the bar. You are within easy reach of the town of Great Bridge that once had a railway line crossing the entrance to the town from the north. This however was no great bridge! The word Great derives from the old English word greot, meaning gravel. At this point the River Tame has a gravelly bed and would have had a crossing giving the town its name Great Bridge. There are amenities here including a traditional market that has been held for centuries at various points in the town.

Designated as a local nature reserve in the year 2000, Sheepwash Local Nature Reserve is edged by a railway track on one side and housing on another. The River Tame flows through the area from south to north on the west side of the park and feeds a series of pools. Here you will see part of 'The River Tame Way'. The water is much cleaner now and these wetlands have proven to be a haven for wild birds and wild flowers. The site is maintained by volunteers and is a superb example of nature reclaiming what was once a heavily industrialised area. Sheepwash Lane gets its name from the sheep that once grazed in the meadows of the River Tame and so literally had a sheepwash for the herd. The geology of the area left it open for the exploitation of minerals through mining or pit digging and gave rise to founding industries requiring coal, gravel and marl. This now tranquil setting that lives on the edges of civilisation was once the site of watermills, iron foundries, busy canals, railways and brickworks.

Today the general public can wander along a series of paths through trees, around pools and along the River Tame and to areas of marshland and streams. The paths are well signposted and are simple to follow, making for easy exploration.

The canal here is the Birmingham to Wolverhampton Mainline Canal. You will walk through Rose Lane meadows with Rose Lane Pool, and will see the Pumphouse Pool and the north fishing pool as well as John's Lane fishing pool and Groveland Brook.

THE BASICS

Distance: 2 miles / 4km
Gradient: Level
Severity: Easy
Time: 1 hr
Stiles: None
Map: OS Explorer 219 (Wolverhampton & Dudley)
Path description: Variable: gravel and earth
Start point: Near the Tame Bridge public house. (GR SO 975921)
Parking: On street (Sheepwash Lane, B4166) and is close to bus routes (DY4 7JB)
Toilets: Nearest is the Tame Bridge or nearby town centre
Dogs: Allowed but site rules need to be adhered to
Refreshments: The Tame Bridge

SHEEPWASH NATURE RESERVE

1. The walk begins opposite a street signed Ballfields and begins to the right of the Tame Bridge pub on Tame Road as you face the pub. The path is overgrown, but persist as this will lead you to the brookside walk. The path opens out onto a well-defined pathway with a tarmac undersurface.

2. Walk towards a pylon where you will see a barred gate in front of you with a nature reserve information sign. Here you will learn about this former industrial site. On the right will be Morrison Road. Go through a gate and past a fingerpost, continuing towards a bridge network. Continue along the main path ignoring the bridge. Walk along the main path between two large pools, taking time to observe the wonderful reclaimed countryside. On the left you will see sluice gates that balance the water levels in the pools. There are paths around the pools but for this walk we will stay on the main path.

3. Bear right and continue along a broad path keeping the brook on your left until you reach a bridge. Take time to stop here. There is a roadside access at this point should you need it via a gate. This will be John's Lane. Take time to spot wild flowers and insects before turning around and retracing your steps back to the main bridge. There is a railway line that runs parallel to the brook and path so the silence will be broken from time to time!

4. Along this section there is great opportunity for photographing wild flowers and indeed painting them if you are an artist. At the main bridge turn right and right again to walk between the two pools. This path runs parallel with the path you have just returned along. Continue through two red and white marker poles. There will be a pool and a rustic fence on your left with young oak, ash and hawthorn trees in evidence. On your right will be the brook. With the pool on your left continue along a broad path. On the left is an information board with reserve rules and regulations. Ignore the first path on the left and continue on the main left turn, which will bend sharply to right.

5. At a fingerpost marked Great Bridge 1440m and Viewpoint 220m turn left along a broad grass path towards Great Bridge. There are residential properties on your right and hedgerows on your left. There is a slight camber along this path so tread carefully!

6. After some time you will have meadows on your left and a main route that takes you back to the roadside. Turn sharp left here through some trees and at a T-junction turn right, continuing on narrower path to your right along the poolside. After a small rise rejoin the broad gravel path turning right towards a fingerpost.

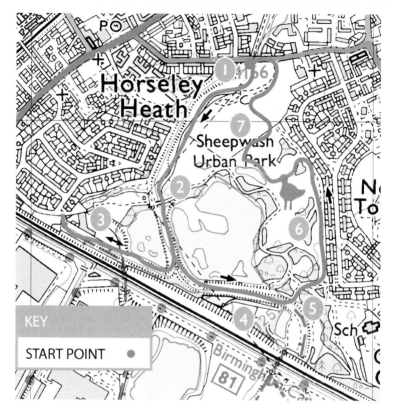

Turn right here signposted Great Bridge, bear left to another fingerpost and at this point continue straight on along the main gravel path. At the next junction ignore the path to the left.

7.   On your right-hand side you will see a rock structure marked 'The Tame Way'. Turn around and return to a bend taking a less defined path to your right. Go through a gate to another broad path. Take a right-hand turn along the broad path. Return to the rock structure on your right, keeping the pylon on your left. Follow the main broad path between red and white poles towards the roadside. There will be a fingerpost on your right but walk towards a turnstile-type gateway. Go through the gate and turn left along the main road to return to the Tame Bridge pub.

MOORCROFT WOOD

The walk begins off Hawkswood Drive, which is a turning signposted for the reserve off Bull Lane (accessible from the A41) where you will find parking in a layby or on the street near to the reserve visitor centre. The site is accessed via a gate just to the left of the building and on your left you will find an information board.

The walk takes you through the woods that once belonged to Moxley isolation hospital, or 'The Sanna' as it was known locally. This hospital was used to treat sufferers of tuberculosis, smallpox and cholera and gave patients a green space to rest from the rigours of the polluted air that would be heavy with soot from the highly industrialised area that surrounded it. The hospital eventually closed in 1995.

Farming and small-scale mining were sited here from at least Roman times right up until the Industrial Revolution took over, extracting iron ore and coal from the site in industrial quantities throughout the 18th and 19th centuries. The minerals found here were combined with local limestone that went into pig iron production at the Moorcroft Ironworks. By 1904 these practices had ceased due to the mines flooding and being too expensive to operate. The hospital was built on the then derelict land.

Sand and clay deposits overlaid the coal and iron and gave rise to brickworks including Murby's industrial blue brick works on the north-eastern side of the reserve. Evidence of these bricks can still be found in some of the canal bridge structures.

Leisure and pleasure fishing is popular here, making use of the large pool, but there are also many shallow pools across the site edged with 'klinker' rocks. The 'klinker' is a by-product of the iron industry and now provides a good habitat for newts and other amphibians. There are several species of wildfowl and if you fancy a mid-evening walk on the warmer nights of summer you may see some of the resident bats including the water bat or Daubenton's bat, known for its low swoops gathering insects that swarm just above the water's surface.

Along the canal there is 'Wardy's Works', a clay pot manufacturer and local employer and some of the most beautiful reclaimed landscape I believe this region has to offer. There are many species of flora and fauna as the walk leads us along the route of Bradley locks and the Walsall Canal. The site houses broad-leafed trees and was originally planted with false acacia and sycamore trees.

THE BASICS

Distance: 3 miles / 6km
Gradient: Some inclines and steps
Severity: Moderate
Time: 1½ hrs
Stiles: None
Map: OS Explorer 219 (Wolverhampton & Dudley)
Path description: Gravel and earth
Start point: Moorcroft Environment Centre. (GR SO 969950)
Parking: On street and is close to bus routes. (WS10 8GA)
Toilets: None
Dogs: Allowed but site rules need to be adhered to
Refreshments: None

MOORCROFT WOOD WALK

1. Enter the reserve through the gate with
    the information board on your left and the
    reserve centre on your right. Follow the main
    path right and turn right at the T-junction
    along a tarmac path. At a small junction
    follow the yellow arrow marker straight on
    to a T-junction. Follow the marker left to
    another junction of paths. At the next post
    walk straight on, following the arrow, up a
    slight incline. There is a metal railed fence
    on the right and on the left you will see glimpses of the pool.

2. At a left turn continue on a gravel path ignoring the next yellow arrow marker. There
    is a pylon on your right and an access gate to the canalside. Go through the gate
    and on your left you will see a canal bridge. Cross the bridge and turn left onto the
    towpath. Take time here to get views along the canal, its wildfowl and flora and
    fauna. Continue beneath Bull Lane Bridge walking towards and under the Holyhead
    Road and Darlaston Road Bridges. At a small towpath bridge turn right around it and
    left to rejoin the main canal path. Continue to the ornate Heathfield Bridge.

3. As you walk off the bridge to your left, keep the factory on your left, walk along the
    tarmac path and you will see a large pool. Keep the pool on your left and walk anti-
    clockwise along a section of the pool to a path through the grass on your right. Walk
    along the path and turn left onto the towpath to walk back along the canal to the
    junction with the reserve.

4. At the ornate metalwork bridge cross the canal to the gate at the access to the
    reserve. Take a right fork through a white top railed gate and take a path leading to
    the right. On the right you will see a pool. Follow the gravel path passing a rustic post
    on the right. Continue along the main path and bear left as you see the pool on your
    left. Bear left on the path. Duck under the partially fallen tree and walk up a steep
    incline towards a mesh fence. Descend a flight of sleeper railed steps. At the rustic
    post turn left affording views across the pool.

5. Follow tarmac path around to the right. Continue along the poolside where there are
    a series of benches. Follow a tarmac path to the right with an information board on
    your left. Follow the natural path on your left that takes you to a broader well-defined
    natural path. Turn left and follow the yellow arrow marker, keeping the railing to the
    right and the pool on the left, where you'll walk back to the canal bridge. There are
    many opportunities to catch glimpses of the pool through the trees.

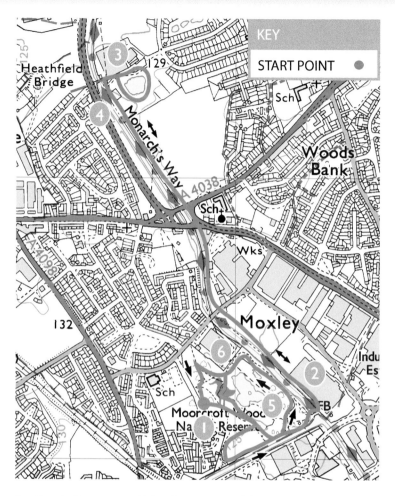

6. Re-enter the reserve and follow the path to the left following the canal branch with a small pool on your right. Follow the long straight path. Continue past the benches on your right and walk along to a narrow access point through a white top rail fence on your right. Ascend the path with housing on your left walking along the path ignoring the yellow markers. Stay on the main tarmac path and turn left, keeping the houses in sight on your left. Ignore the first left turning through a gate. This is the Environment Centre turning. Take the next left through a gate that takes you to the roadside. Turn left and the visitor centre is in front of you. The woods extend across the road. Return to the start point.

WEDNESBURY

THE TOWN OF WEDNESBURY LIES TOWARDS THE NORTHERN
EDGE OF THE BLACK COUNTRY AND ONCE BELONGED
TO SOUTH STAFFORDSHIRE BEFORE THE METROPOLITAN
BOROUGH OF SANDWELL WAS FORMED IN 1974.

The town is easily identified from some distance by the two church steeples rising up on the hill. One spire is the copper spire of St Mary on the Hill that was built in 1872 to the design of Gilbert Blount. The other is the spire of St Bartholomew's Church, first mentioned in the early 13th century and believed to be considerably older than the 1210 dateline. Both churches sit prominently upon Church Hill, believed to be the site of an Iron Age hill fort. St Bartholomew's Church houses fine examples of stained glass windows designed by Charles Kempe, many containing his 'wheatsheaf' signature.

The name Wednesbury derives from the Norse god Woden and byri, meaning barrow or fortification. Ethelflaeda, daughter of King Alfred, turned Wednesbury into a fortified town to defend the lands from the Danes. It is believed that there were two major battles here in the 6th and 8th centuries during the Anglo-Saxon period and it is one of the few places in this country that has direct reference to the god Woden, who 'rode' across the skies on his warhorse Sleipnir.

Wednesbury was situated on the southern edge of a great forest that stretched across Staffordshire, remnants of which can be seen at Canock Chase. During the formative years of the town and through the medieval period industry thrived in the area. Small-scale iron and pottery industries used trees to fire charcoal ovens or furnaces and quickly depleted the forest through industry and habitation. Wedgebury Ware was the much sought after utility products for those who could afford the fine kitchen and tablewares produced by using the town's rich layers of clay. Red and yellow clays were used for drinking vessels and bowls. White Monway clay went into making tobacco smoking pipes. By the 18th century farming was still a source of employment though coal mining, and the continued building of canals and eventually rail sculpted the landscape as it is today.

Wednesbury is still identifiable as an old market town and retains many interesting buildings including the library and art gallery. Brunswick Park is situated along the Wood Green Road and was designed as the 'green lung' for the town during the heavy industrialisation of the area. The park now offers continued leisure facilities in a much needed and loved urban green space.

THE BASICS

Distance: 3 miles / 5km
Gradient: Steep in places
Severity: Moderate walk
Time: 1 hour 10 mins
Stiles: None
Map: OS Explorer 219 (Wolverhampton & Dudley)
Path description: Tarmac
Start point: St Bartholemew's Church, Church Hill. (GR SO 987951)
Parking: Near St Bartholemew's Church. (WS10 9DE)
Toilets: Town centre
Dogs: Allowed but need to be on lead
Refreshments: Town centre

WEDNESBURY WALK

1. The walk begins at St Bartholomew's Church on Church Hill. Inside the church there is a cock lectern believed to be unique in the fact that this depicts a retired fighting cock. Its spurs and metal comb are missing from the carving, which suggests at some point peace comes to us all! Cock fighting was prevalent in this area and gave rise to the ballad 'Wedgbury Cocking'. With your back to the church look out across the green  space to your right for views of Dudley Castle in the distance. Walk downhill along Ethelflaeda Terrace towards the main road where you will turn left.

2. Do not cross the A461; over the road, however, was the site of Earp's Lane. Yes, Wyatt Earp of Wild West fame was from these parts! You will pass The Bellwether pub on the right. At Brunswick Terrace look along it and you will see a curious wall splitting the roadway/walkway in two. The other side is known as Squires Walk and was a private footpath to the manor. Continue to the Andrew Carnegie subscribed library and the Cenotaph. Across the road you will see an old Georgian brick wall. On the other side of this wall is an old town well head. The whole area was fed water by the River Tame, giving rise to Oakeswell Street, Wellcroft Avenue and Spring Head. Some of the wells were for public use, others private!

3. Cross the road at the light-controlled crossing after Kendrick Street, turn left and cross Knowles Street and Foley Street to enter historic Brunswick Park on your right. Enter the park and take the path on the left. Stay on the path parallel to the main road. On your left is the ornate old clock tower dedicated to the town to commemorate the coronation of King George V. Take a left fork in the path to the main road and turn right to Wood Green Cemetery. This cemetery contains memorials to some local notables as well as commonwealth war graves. Return to the park with views of the old pump station beyond. Follow the path to the right and towards the bandstand with its terraced landscape. Walk past the bandstand, taking the path to your right. Turn right uphill past the gym equipment on your left. Turn immediately right and follow the path past tennis courts to Brunswick Park Road.

4. Turn right on Brunswick Park Road and walk to the junction with Hydes Road. Turn left and cross the road where safe to do so and then turn right along Corporation Street. Cross Oakeswell Street and Wharfedale Street. Continue to Ridding Lane and turn right. Walk into Market Place and the old clock tower. This was the site of public meetings especially during the 1913 tubeworkers' strike. To the left is

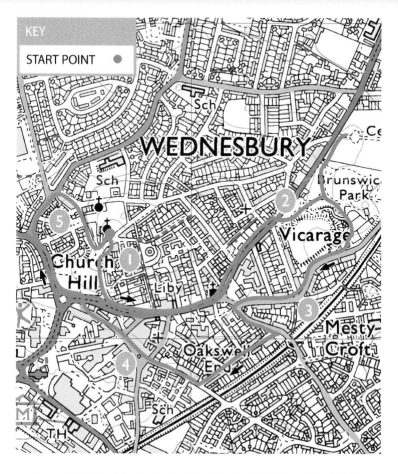

Lower High Street, leading to the site of the old Chartists meeting hall. Across from you is the Shambles where animals were butchered for consumption from market sales. Walk along Upper High Street turning right up a small alley with steps to main road. Turn left and cross at the light-controlled crossing. Turn left along the main road and then right into Trouse Lane. The churches should be to your right and the stainless steel Sleipnir sculpture from the Metro leaping towards the town in the mid-distance to your left.

5. Take the second right turn into Whitley Street. Cross Park Street and go onto Manor House Road. Turn right onto Hall End. On your left is the infamous Blue Ball pub which still has the remains of a fighting cock pit in its back yard! Turn right at the top of Hall End and return to St Bartholomew's Church and the start point.

SOT'S HOLE

Sot's Hole is situated just off Church Vale and is close to Sandwell General Hospital and Sandwell Valley. There are regular buses to the area and parking is easy.

Follow the signs to Eaton Valley Primary School where there is a car park to your right for the Sot's Hole Nature reserve. This short walk can also be taken in conjunction with the two other Sandwell Valley walks contained in this book.

As a nature reserve Sot's Hole is a rare example of ancient woodland and marshland green space in the post-industrial Black Country. Recent research on the site has found flint instruments and burnt mounds that date back to the Bronze Age. Centuries of farming and industrial uses of the land are also evident in the archaeology of this intriguing landscape. The original pools (now marshy hollows) have been cleared of overgrowth and dams and sluices can now be seen once again. These were needed to help supply local mills with water along the meandering route of the River Tame.

In 1760 maps of the locale named this area Chambers Wood, though the name Sot's Hole preceded that date and is derived from a local term for a drunkard, or sot. The Bear and Ragged Staff pub was owned by the said sot from 1719 to 1769, the pub being situated in the dip of Dagger Lane! Somewhat confusingly the reserve is also known locally as Bluebell Wood and Bunny's Wood for self-explanatory reasons.

The habitat at Sot's Hole provides special conditions for particular insect life and other wildlife including water voles, woodpeckers and foxes. The wet nature of this ancient woodland is also host to plants like the marsh thistle and water horse-tail.

Access to the reserve is via Church Vale, where you will find an ornate kissing gate a few yards to the left of the school drive as you face it. The reserve is always open so access to and departure from it is not time sensitive.

The reserve boasts disabled access along some of its broad paths although some of the minor routes can be overgrown in summer. This walk combines the reserve with the edge of Sandwell Country Park and is therefore only partially wheelchair friendly. It would be advisable to check access and routes prior to setting off with disabled walkers to avoid any disappointment.

THE BASICS

Distance: 2 miles / 3.5km
Gradient: Slight inclines and some steps
Severity: Easy
Time: 1 hr
Stiles: One
Map: OS Explorer 219 (Wolverhampton & Dudley)
Start point: Kissing gate in Church Vale. (GR SP 011921)
Path description: Variable: rocky, gravel and earth
Parking: Visitor car park, Eaton Valley Primary School. (B71 4BU)
Toilets: none
Dogs: Allowed but site rules need to be adhered to
Refreshments: None

SOT'S HOLE WALK

1. From the kissing gate, walk along the main gravel path passing the 'welcome' marker and continue along a broad path that bends to the left between large holly trees. Take time here to look around. The woodland scent here in summer is intense.

2. At the next waymarker follow the direction arrow for Marshland Walk. Take the left fork and cross a small bridge to a narrow path. This is not suitable for wheelchairs. In summer these paths can have overhanging briar and thistle, so please take care. On the left-hand side you will see a carved marker with Marshland Walk carved into it. Continue along the waymarked Marshland Walk. Keep on the main path to a small, gated bridge which is near to a very small weir. There is a bench close by if needed.

3. Follow the defined hard-core path slightly to the right, ignoring a path to the left. Turn left at the main path junction and marker that will put you onto the Bluebell Walk. Turn left at 'Pond' marker; this route will take you to a viewing platform to observe the pond and its ecosystem. Rejoin the main path and follow a reddish brick-based path turning left at the 'Pond' marker and continuing along a grey path through the trees. At a carved waymarker there is a flight of steps to your right. Ignore these steps and turn left to follow a narrow path through the trees towards the golf course.

4. The path turns away from the golf course and along the stream. This area is wet but the path is easily visible. Turn to the right and take care stepping over fallen trees. These trees provide habitat for fungi and insects. Continue along the path to the main gravel path where you will turn left.

5. Continue along the main path until you reach the flight of steps on your right. This time follow the marker to 'Country Park'. On reaching the top of the steps there is open meadow in front of you. You are now entering Sandwell Valley. Turn left, keeping Sot's Hole on your left, and follow the main path along the edge of the field on your right. You will have glimpsing views of the reserve.

6. Follow the path to the right and approach a gate. Do not go through this gate. Turn left at a post marked 13 and follow the waymarked green arrow. This route takes you

through a fern-lined pathway. In summer this area is teeming with butterflies. Follow the path to the right keeping the field on your right and then turn right at the corner of the field. Turn right again at the next corner. Turn right by crossing a stile gate on your right to a defined path through the field. Sot's Hole is now visible. Walk through the galvanised metal gate and follow the main broad route round to left. Stay on the main route heading towards farm buildings. Ignore any turnings off this path.

7. Follow the path around a right-hand bend, where it will now ascend towards a main road. Turn right before you get to the gates. Continue along the fields with a school on your left. The path descends towards the entrance to Sot's Hole. Ignore the path on your left and turn right at the corner of the field to the information board. Turn left and descend the flight of steps. Turn left at the foot of steps and continue past the 'Pond' marker and follow the 'Way Out' marker. At the next marker take the left-hand route towards the main road. Go through the gates and turn left onto Dagger Lane and then first left to the car park and start point.

SANDWELL VALLEY

Close to Junction 1 of the M5 motorway and within ten to fifteen minutes' walk of the town of West Bromwich, Sandwell Valley has most of the amenities needed for a family day out. Access to the site is signposted off Dagger Lane via Salter's Lane.

Sandwell Valley Nature Reserve is an award-winning Green Flag initiative catering for outdoor interests and for all ages and abilities. Some of the site is geared towards family and child-friendly activities but for those who like things a little quieter and less hectic, you can, within a few minutes, be in open countryside or walking along tree-canopied pathways.

At the end of a long driveway there is ample parking to the right or, preferably for where this walk begins, there is another car park straight ahead. Just along from the car park is Sandwell Park Farm, which is open from 10am to 4.30pm and is home to a small exhibition, farm shop, tea room and farmyard. There is a small admission charge to access the amenities there. The enterprise itself is a fully restored and working Victorian farm with grazing meadows and yard and is Grade II listed for preservation purposes.

The whole site consists of 660 acres of parkland, farmland, pools and streams. Popular with walkers and cyclists alike the whole site is well maintained and has much in the way of accommodating wheelchair access to some prime beauty spots. Fishing and birdwatching are also popular in and around the extensive pools where access to the water's edge is safe and well defined. Birds range from winter ducks to summer warblers depending on the season, and many migratory birds and wildfowl including teal, cormorant and heron can also be found resting and feeding.

The site once housed a priory and the pools are part of the farming that the monks used to feed themselves. Today the ruins of the old priory are all that remain of this 13th-century settlement of monks that was built close to the Sand Well that supplied fresh water to the priory.

The building fell into disrepair and was closed by the order of Cardinal Wolsey. The building went into further disrepair until Sandwell Hall was built in 1705, which utilised some of the external walls of the priory. In turn the hall was finally demolished in 1928 to leave the site pretty much as it is today.

THE BASICS

Distance: 4 miles / 6.5km
Gradient: Steep and slippery in places
Severity: Moderate walk
Time: 1¾ hrs
Stiles: None
Map: OS Explorer 219 (Wolverhampton & Dudley)
Path description: Variable: tarmac, gravel and earth
Start point: Sandwell Park Farm. (GR SP 018913)
Parking: Sandwell Park Farm. (B71 4BG)
Toilets: At visitor centre
Dogs: Allowed but site rules need to be adhered to
Refreshments: At visitor centre

SANDWELL VALLEY WALK

1. The walk begins on the main car park at Sandwell Park Farm and the walk is clearly signposted Priory Woods. Walk through a galvanised turnstile-type gate. Continue along a tarmac path past a shady reserve of benches and sculptures on your left. At a fingerpost follow the direction for Swan Pool. Ignore any turnings on the left and follow the path over the M5 motorway and take the first left along a broad concrete path. To the left of you is the M5 and to your right is woodland.

2. Continue along the path until on your right there is a kissing gate. Walk through the gate to Priory Woods. In a short time there is the Ice House Pool and you continue along the path with the pool on your right. There is a marker on your left marked 5 where you will find a viewing platform. Keep on gravel path and bend slightly to the right, continuing to a fork in the pathway where you will go straight on the Cascade Pool. Follow the path to the right between pools with Cascade Pool on your left following the green markers. At a main junction turn right and continue to Priory Woods and the priory. The path is adjacent to the golf course. Go through a kissing gate and continue to the information board relating to the ruins of the old priory. Here you will get views of this ancient and archaeologically important site. A little further along the path that takes you around the perimeter of the site you will find the spring of Sand Well that provided water to the priory.

3. Continue along the main path keeping open meadow on your left and ignoring any side turnings or pathways. On your left you will see Swan Pool in the distance. The path will go up a small incline and then cross the road and rejoin the path over the road at kissing gates. Walk along the main tarmac path. Ignore first major left turning. The path will bend to the right where you will see allotments to your right. Take the left turning before you reach the road ahead of you. The path will take you along a grassed pathway with railings and houses on your right. You will now start to climb a hill. Ascend the hill and at the top where a concrete path appears look to

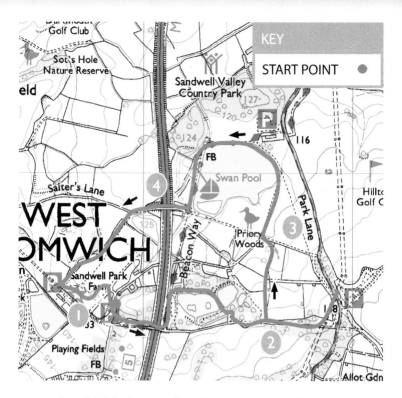

your immediate left where you will see the concrete remains of a World War II anti-aircraft gun post. Take a look at the views towards Birmingham behind and below you before returning along the path to the base of the hill. Turn right at the path and return to the nature reserve grounds. The allotments will be on your left. Continue along the path and cross the road to Priory Woods.

4. On a broad path turn immediate right; the pathway will bend to the left. Stay on the main path; to your right will be Park Lane. At a junction look ahead to Hill Top and left to Swan Pool. Carry straight on along the narrower gravel path. Swan Pool will be across fields on your left. At a T-junction turn right at Swan Pool keeping the pool on your left. Follow the path around the pool. Turn right at a concrete path to take you over the motorway bridge. Turn left to join a tarmac path and follow green and blue route signs. Turn left at a cyclists' information fingerpost. This is through a narrow bricked area with slatted gates. To your right is open meadowland. Follow the path to the right and here you will see the Sandwell Valley recreation area. Follow the tarmac path towards the car park and Sandwell Park Farm buildings and the start point.

FORGE MILL

The Sandwell Valley RSPB Reserve is adjacent to Forge Mill Farm, where you will find a visitor centre serving hot and cold drinks and selling biscuits, gifts, plants and vegetables as well as dairy and other local farm produce. The centre and car park are open from 10 am to 4.30 pm throughout the year.

Please park on the main car park for the reserve as there are two access points along Forge Lane. One is to the farm, which has a very small car park. The site centres around a large lake and has the River Tame flowing through it. It comprises of 660 acres of grassland, woodland, hedgerows and scrub and is home to wide and varied wildlife. There is also an area of marshland with RSPB hides for the serious birdwatcher. At the RSPB centre there are also small wildlife ponds including a newt pond. In spring and summer there are opportunities to see many species of wildflower including southern marsh orchids. The site is also host to many migrating and resident birds as well as butterflies and other insect life.

The site began its industrialisation in the 1700s when it was home to an iron-slitting mill processing iron rods for other local metal industries. There were many mill sites along the River Tame at this point in time. In later years however, the site became a flour mill before the water levels dropped in the area, making it impossible to make use of the once abundant natural resources.

The farm offers opportunities to feed the animals, learn more about farm life and gain experience of the daily tasks involved in operating a fully utilised working farm. It also has a walk around the farm and accompanying farmland where you can witness further the day-to-day running of a venture of this nature. All the staff are friendly and keen to help with any questions or information relating to the site and in summer the farm is home to a maze of maize, where the public are invited to find their way around the twists and turns cut into the crop to produce a living and fun attraction.

If the noise and industry of the farm are too much then peaceful and tranquil walks await!

THE BASICS

Distance: 4 miles / 7km
Gradient: Slight, with some steps
Severity: Moderate walk
Time: 2 hrs
Stiles: None
Map: OS Explorer 219 (Wolverhampton & Dudley)
Path description: Variable: tarmac, gravel and earth
Start point: Sandwell Valley RSPB car park. (GR SP 028927)
Parking: Sandwell Valley RSPB car park. (B71 3SZ)
Toilets: Visitor centre
Dogs: Allowed but site rules need to be adhered to
Refreshments: Visitor centre

FORGE MILL

1. On the main visitor car park and with your back to towards the farm buildings walk to the top left corner where the walk will be signposted 'Forge Mill Lake'. Once through the kissing gate in front of you you will see the lake. Continue along the main path and across a concrete sectioned bridge over the River Tame. Turn left along a broad gravel path with the river on your left and the lake on your right. Continue along this path towards the main road. Walk under the green railway bridge, ignoring any paths off the main one. Before reaching a road bridge turn right along a tarmac path to take you towards Bishop Asbury's Cottage. Turn right across a grassed path through trees and on your left will be access to the main road. Cross where you can and turn left at Malt Shovel public house to find the cottage. If not return along paths towards the road bridge, turning left on the main pathway to retrace your steps along the River Tame Way. Keep the River Tame on your right.

2. Continue along the main tarmac path before turning left at a gravel path just before reaching the green railway bridge; the railway lines will now be on your right. Continue left up a slight incline with the railway track on your right to a right fork and continue through a small gatepost. The path veers to the left. Continue along this path with a mesh fence to your right. This section can be overgrown in summer. Walk through a tree-covered section towards open land and a residential area on your left. Veer right on the path and descend into a wooded area that leads to a car park. From the path turn right and cross a railway bridge, bearing right. At a lay-by follow the footpath to the left of the road. Go through a green gate to the visitor centre, and the RSPB Nature Reserve should be ahead of you. There is plenty of opportunity to sit and picnic here as well as look at the newt pond!

3. Retrace your steps from the RSPB reserve past the newt pond and take the gravel pathway to your right through a corralled section and path to the right to overlook the marsh from a viewing area. Proceed to a flight of steps down on your right to take you to the River Tame Way footpath. Turn left at the bottom of the steps and follow the main path right, keeping the marsh to your right and the river on your left.

4. Walk along the main gravel path where there will be many opportunities to see the marshes to your right. Continue to the concrete bridge that will take you back to the car parks. At Forge Mill Pool turn left and cross the bridge, then turn right across a grassed area to an information board. Enter the main car park.

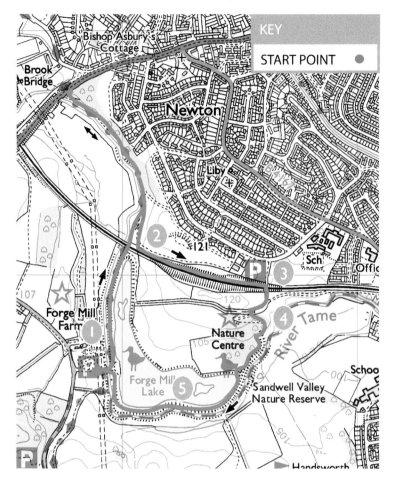

KEY

START POINT ●

5. Follow signposts to the farm and farm car park, passing a play area on your right. Cross the farmyard, being aware that this is a working farm and has moving machinery. The Farm Trail begins with an information board and map at the start of this section. Walk through the gates and follow the main gravel path circular walk. As you walk along here there will be evidence of Environment Agency equipment. Continue following the path around the fields where there are sheep and horses to be seen grazing. Sections of this walk can be boggy even during dry spells. There are further opportunities to see wild flowers and insects. Return to the farm buildings and car parks.

HYDES ROAD POOL

HYDES ROAD POOL IS SITUATED OFF WODEN ROAD SOUTH AND IS ADJACENT TO HYDES ROAD. THE POOL HAS HAD A CHEQUERED EXISTENCE, DRAINING AWAY ALMOST COMPLETELY IN RECENT TIMES DUE TO OPEN-CAST MINING CHANNELLING WATER AWAY.

Over the last twenty years, though, it has become a much-loved feature of Wednesbury and not only provides a rich haven for wildlife and leisure but is also the gateway to the Tame Valley Canal at this point.

A recent housing development now stands on the site of a former college and has to some degree preserved the integrity of the site. The

inter-war estate to the north of the pool is known locally as the 'Golf Links Estate' as this whole area was a golf course from 1908 to 1939. The pool then was known as 'the water hole' as it was a pit dug for extracting fireclay for a nearby brickworks.

The walk begins at the pool and will take us to the Tame Valley Canal and through the post-industrial areas of Balls Hill and Golds Green and up to Ryders Green before returning along the same route. There are plenty of opportunities on this walk to see old factories and early canal bridges that are still grooved by the ropes of towing horses on the canal in both brickwork and cast iron curbings. It will take us through the Tame Valley Junction where there is now a mooring for residential boats and also to the site that once housed the three giant cooling towers for Ocker Hill power station, a landmark that you will see in any old photographs from the area prior to the mid-1980s.

There is still a waterway romance along these old stretches of the canals and some still conduct the smells of forges and other industrial processes still in use today, though much scaled down from its industrial past.

For those interested in industrial heritage sites, Great Bridge and Horsely Heath were where the factory sites of Horseley Bridge and Thomas Piggot once stood. Their reputation globally was immense. They built the first iron steam ship, the Aaron Manby, as well as supplying bridges and engineering to the rest of the world. Many of the local canal bridges were made here. You will also find the gates to a lesser known glass works, Stevens and Williams, which produced industrial standard glass fittings from lighting through to cathode ray tubes during World War II.

THE BASICS

Distance: 4 miles / 8km
Gradient: Slight
Severity: Easy walk
Time: 2 hrs
Stiles: None
Map: OS Explorer 219 (Wolverhampton & Dudley)
Path description: Variable: tarmac, gravel and earth
Start point: Woden Road South, near junction with Hydes Road. (GR SO 996945)
Parking: On street and close to bus routes. (WS10 0DH)
Toilets: None
Dogs: Allowed but site rules need to be adhered to
Refreshments: None

1. The walk starts in Woden Road South opposite the Hydes Road traffic island. Walk along to the side of the pool keeping the pool on your left and Woden Road South on your right. Walk along the grass to a ring of birch trees where there is a wildlife information board. Continue to a tarmac path and turn left.

2. Cross a small concrete bridge over the River Tame and continue through a housing estate and along Tame Crossing until you reach the canal at Balls Hill. Go through a staggered gate and cross the canal bridge, turning right along the towpath, and walk under Holloway Road bridge. Continue along the towpath and walk under the Metro line bridge which takes the local tram network over the canal. Walk towards a smaller bridge on the towpath. This is Jones Bridge. Beware as it is very low and you will have to dip down a bit!

3. There is an opportunity along this section to see some of the old factories that lined the canals. You can only imagine how busy these canals would have been with freight in days gone by. You can still smell oil/diesel rising from the water on warm days here. Continue under Gold's Hill Bridge towards the Tame Valley Junction. On the right-hand side is the power station that was once served by three cooling towers. In recent times two concrete towers replaced them, housing Olympus engines like the ones that once powered Concorde. On the left you will see local horses tethered in the grassland. Look down to your left to see the River Tame flowing under the canal. The water is very dark here, reflecting its industrial past.

4. Walk under Ocker Hill Road Bridge, through a gate to a fingerpost. Here you will see a canal network junction. Follow the path and cross the canal at a black and white bridge. Look along the canal to see other bridges that stretch across the waterway. Turn left and follow the sign to Ryders Green. Cross the towpath bridge remaining on the same side of the towpath and look to your right to the boat moorings and the training station for the electricity board. This site also has a private pool which was a clay pit for brickmaking in more industrial times. Cross a towpath bridge, remaining on same side of canal to Moors Mill Lane bridge. There is often a smell of foundry along here. Approach the red-brick Hempole Bridge, which has a cast iron sign mounted upon it bearing the date 1825 in Roman numerals. Walk under Hempole Railway Bridge; there are drainage troughs across the towpath here so please take care. Have a look at the brickwork. Some of the bricks are grooved from the ropes of towing horses pulling boats through for over 200 years!

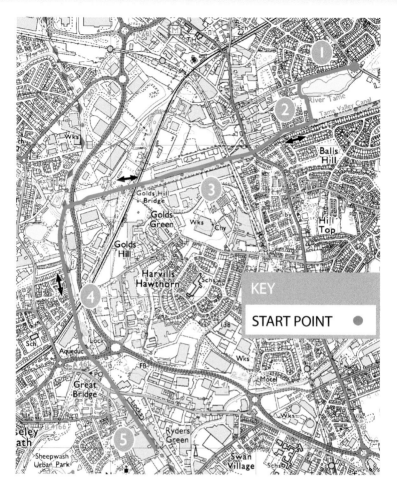

5. Continue around a left-hand bend to a lock. With care you can see the cast iron rubbing curbs that were used to protect the brickwork from the boats. Continue to Ryders Green Locks Bridge. Walk under the bridge and continue to a red brick bridge which is Brick House Lane Bridge. Look at the ceiling of the bridge, where you'll see its ironwork construction with eight concave features in the design. We are now at Great Bridge and to the rear of the market. Continue along the towpath to the newly built Wellington Bridge. Look to your right where you will see an access point to a retail park that has food and other amenities. Turn around here and retrace your steps back to Hydes Road Pool, remembering to turn right when you reach the Tame Valley Junction.

PARK LIME PITS

Park Lime Pits is situated off Park Road and is accessible from the designated car park. It lies between Walsall Arboretum to the south and Chasewater to the north and is linked to them by canal.

You will pass two public houses on the way to the lane that takes you to the nature reserve car park. The first is The Boathouse and the second The Manor Arms, which has canalside views, dates back to the dawn of the 12th century and has had many subsequent rebuilds and add-ons. This former farmhouse became  an alehouse in the 19th century serving the boat crews on the nearby canal.

Originally the site was a limestone quarry supplying lime to the iron industry via the canal network. When the mining ceased in the mid-19th century the Victorians planted beech trees and allowed the quarry to fill with water. The alkalinity of the soil here gives rise to the diverse array of wildlife that boasts over three hundred species of plants. Running through the site is Adam's Brook, which among other creatures contains the rare white-clawed crayfish. The site is also home to over a hundred species of birds as well as Daubenton's bats.

This walk will take you from the reserve and along the Rushall Canal from close proximity to the remains of Rushall Hall (literally Rush Hall and of 12th-century Anglo-Saxon origin) to the beautifully landscaped Walsall Arboretum. En route we will pass other local areas of wildlife including walking along the canal, cutting through Hayhead Wood and walking alongside Calderfields Golf Club.

The walk will take you to the site of Walsall Arboretum. The walks around the parkland are varied and so we will not include them here. They are for you to add to or revisit when you're next in the area. The parkland was opened in 1874 and consisted of lakes and lodges as well as a boathouse, summerhouses and promenades. Until recently the Arboreteum held its annual and then biennial illuminations when in Autumn the parklands were lit up with active lighting displays similar to Blackpool but on a smaller scale. The illuminations finished in 2009 due to financial issues, ending a tradition that started in 1875 with candlelit walkways. It houses many amenities today including play areas, bowling greens and a golf course. Hatherton Lake also gives the opportunity for a bit of boating with vessels for hire.

THE BASICS

Distance: 6 miles / 10km
Gradient: Mainly level but with some steps
Severity: Moderate walk
Time: 2½ hrs
Stiles: None
Map: OS Explorer 220 (Birmingham)
Path description: Gravel and tarmac
Start point: Car park at Park Lime Pits. (GR SK 032001)
Parking: Park Lime Pits car park. (WS4 1LG)
Toilets: Nearby public houses
Dogs: Allowed but site rules need to be adhered to
Refreshments: Public houses

PARK LIME PITS WALK

1. In the car park, park in one of the bays and access the reserve from there. Walk back across a cattle grid and turn right through a gate with an information board on the left. Continue along a gravel path where you'll see the canal to your left. Follow a path to the right. At a waymarker follow yellow arrows for  Beacon Way. Continue along a main path to a small culvert on the left. A little further along is a working farm. Turn right on the path and immediate right to a blue plaque describing the lime industry from the 15th century. Walk up a broad gravel path following the path of the stream to your right. The pits will now come into view.

2. Cross a small, boarded link-way between the pools. Turn left at a yellow arrow marker and up a flight of boarded steps. Here there are elevated views of the lime pit pools. Go straight on at the next arrow over a small, boarded bridge and down some steps. At the next waymarker follow 'lime pit walk' and ignore the yellow arrow. Keep following the contour of the pits along the designated path. Descend boarded steps and follow a timber railed route.

3. Continue along the main path over a boarded section. Keep the pits to your left and then turn left over a two-planked bridge. Continue along the main path, which rises to a chicane of boarded steps that follow the undulation of the land. Turn slight right and immediate left past the blue sign for the pits. Before reaching the car park turn right through a kissing gate and right onto to the canal.

4. Walk along towpath to Riddian Bridge, taking time to look at the cast iron rubbing curbs on the bridge where they are grooved with ropes from towing horses. Continue along the towpath under Longwood Bridge, passing Longwood Boat Club on the right. Head towards a flight of locks that step down onto the towpath. There is an abundance of lilies along this section of canal in August. Walk past Calderfields Golf Course and continue under Moat Bridge and Sutton Road Bridge. Just before the Sutton Road Bridge on your right there is a path* through the hedge should you wish to go to Walsall Arboretum (see below). Continue under Gillity Bridge to see more lilies, gardens and wildlife to number three lock where there is a lock-keeper's cottage. At Five Ways Bridge turn around and return to Sutton Road Bridge. Just along from the bridge is a cut-through path on your left through a hedge*; the canal will be on your right. This will take you to the Arboretum. If you do not wish to go to the Arboretum continue along the canal towpath and skip instruction 5.

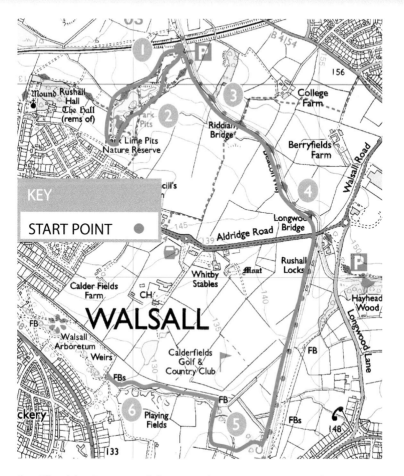

5. *The Arboretum car park is accessed across a green space known as the Arboretum Extension. Follow the broad mowed path and continue under an old oak tree, keeping a line of properties to your left. Take a right turning just past the oak tree and continue across grassland. Continue straight on and follow the pathway as it bears left. Stay on a broad path that eventually becomes a gravel path. Cross a short, boarded section over a ditch and continue straight on to a car park. Retrace your steps to the canal and turn left.

6. Continue along the towpath until you come to Riddian Bridge. Once past the bridge continue a little way before turning left onto a tarmac path signposted as a public footpath. This pathway returns you to the car park start point.

TIPTON & BIRMINGHAM CANAL

ALL AROUND THE BLACK COUNTRY YOU WILL FIND
EVIDENCE OF ITS INDUSTRIAL PAST. ITS LEGACY IS STILL TO
BE FOUND EVEN TODAY. CRUMBLING FACTORY SITES AND
DESERTED INDUSTRIES TELL THE STORY OF THIS REGION ONCE
KNOWN AS THE WORKSHOP OF THE WORLD. THIS WALK
WILL TAKE YOU AROUND PART OF WHAT IS ARGUABLY THE
CRUCIBLE OF THE BLACK COUNTRY.

If you take your time and dig a little
for the story being told by this much-
disturbed landscape you will find it
a treasure trove of inventions and
industrial archaeology.

The walk begins at Tipton (the Domesday
Book referred to it as Tibbington)
railway station. There is easy parking
in the town off Owen Street, where you
will find several car parks, and the town
is also served extensively by road and
rail public transport services.

From the canal bridge close to Tipton station you will get your first glimpse of The
Birmingham Canal. The Birmingham Canal was a major arterial route for freight traffic to
and from the town and its branch canals circle Tipton in pretty much the way a ring road
encircles a town today. The Tipton Green Branch was completed in and around 1805 and
had three locks to contend with gradient changes. The nearby area of Bloomfields gives
a thought to the region's ancient industrial heritage where iron ore or blooms were mined
and smelted in the Saxon period.

Turning round and looking behind you across the road you will see Caggy's boatyard
which opened in 1960 and forms the entrance to the Toll End Communication Canal It
continues to this day to be known locally as Caggy's even though the business is under
new ownership.

The structural decline of canals and their use for freight continued with the building of
road and rail, which led to a century of demise from the late 19th century through to the
mid-20th century.

This decline in fortunes for the canal led to this section being drained and in-filled in 1976. The waters are a lot clearer now, but they still whisper of the characters and industries that they served from the dawn of the Industrial Revolution. When walking along the towpaths please be aware of tripping hazards but do look out for carp as they can easily be seen dodging the floats and fishing hooks of local anglers!

THE BASICS

Distance: 4 miles / 6.5km
Gradient: Slight
Severity: Easy
Time: 1¾ hrs
Stiles: None
Map: OS Explorer 219 (Wolverhampton & Dudley)
Path description: Variable: tarmac, gravel and earth
Start point: Tipton railway station. (GR SO 956925)
Parking: Car parks in Tipton town centre. (DY4 8ET)
Toilets: None
Dogs: Allowed but site rules need to be adhered to
Refreshments: None

1. Enter the canalside from the bridge close to the railway station. The path will be to your right and leads down a brick path to a gravel path and under Wood Street footbridge. To your right is an area known as 'The Cracker', where limestone was burned for use in the iron industry. At factory locks marked number 3, have a look at the small but interesting ornate cast iron bridge. Walk under Factory Road Bridge and past number one lock to join the towpath at the old gauging station built in 1873 where narrowboats carrying cargo were given official weight marks on their sides which indicated the weight of their load as they passed toll houses and made their deliveries. Alongside the gauging station is the Boatman's Mission that was built some twenty years later. The mission provided spiritual guidance and food and drinks that were not alcoholic! It also helped provide some education for children as they travelled along the waterways. Times were tough on the boats, where many a cargo delivery fee was sunk in the local ale houses!

2. Continue under the Old Factory Road Bridge and Factory Road Bridge where you'll see the Barge and Barrel public house. At Factory Road Bridge walk over Old Factory Road Bridge by doubling back on yourself to join the old main line canal. Walk through a gate and approach a right-hand bend. Here on your right you'll pass the Neptune Health Centre. In front of you is Coronation Gardens, which houses the memorial to prize fighter William Perry, 'the Tipton Slasher'. On your left is the Fountain Pub, which was once run by Perry. Walk under Owen Street Bridge and continue on to a brick pathway.

3. You are now entering the area of Tipton Green that became the site of a battlefield as Parliamentarian forces attacked nearby Dudley Castle in 1644. During the Industrial Revolution Tipton Green became highly industrialised and densely populated, rising to around 8,000 people in the 1840s. Iron-founders A. Harper and Sons occupied the site from 1822, the factory diversifying from supplying car parts to building cars, including the now collectible Perry Car. Continue along a cobbled towpath to a brick pathway. Enter Beehive Walk and on the right is an access point in a brick wall. Walk down the steps and through a gate under Tipton Green Bridge. On the right is the

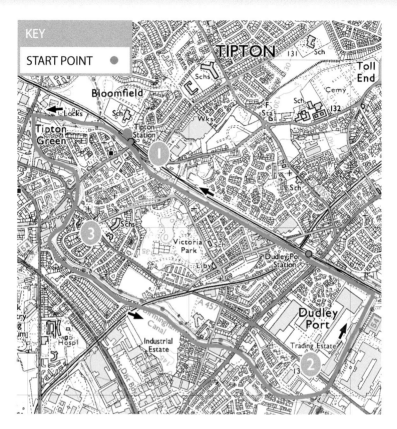

site of a roundhouse toll booth. Further on to your right is canal access to the Black Country Museum, once the route for the Dudley Tunnel. Follow the path left under Pitchfork Bridge and Coneygre Railway Bridges. Walk through a staggered gate to a tarmac path to Randals Bridge. Walk around the bridge and under Keir Bridge. Carry on along the towpath, turning left to join the Netherton Canal. Walk under Groveland Road Bridge to Toll End Bridge where you'll have views to Sheepwash Lane Nature Reserve. Turn right over a bridge and then turn left over Toll End Works bridge so the railway line is now on your right. The towpath here is narrow and will eventually take you over Dudley Port Bridge and Park Lane East Bridge. On your left is a view to the old Tipton Library built by Andrew Carnegie, which opened in March 1903. Continue under Watery Lane Bridge and BCN 1880 bridges. Walk over another bridge and look to your right to view Caggy's Boatyard. Continue to Owen Street and Station Bridge to end the walk.

MERRION'S WOOD

THIS SHORT WALK MAY NOT TAKE YOU ALONG ANY GREAT DISTANCE BUT IT DOES EFFECTIVELY TAKE YOU BACK IN TIME. MERRION'S WOOD IS REPRESENTATIVE OF OLD ENGLAND BEFORE THE RAVAGES OF THE INDUSTRIAL REVOLUTION TOOK PLACE THAT EVENTUALLY SCARRED THE FACE OF MUCH OF THE 'WORKSHOP' MIDLANDS.

It is described as a 'cathedral of trees' and contains very old oak and beech trees. The wood is a natural gem just three miles from Walsall town centre. Parking is limited and is situated at Merrion's Wood Lodge. Look for a gravel driveway parallel to the main A34 Birmingham Road dual carriageway. It is accessed via the junction with Skip Lane. The entrance to the site is not obvious but if you walk towards the lodge you will see the signposted gated entrance to the left of the building.

Merrion's Wood is an all-year-round place to visit and boasts seasonal changes in its natural beauty with its bluebells and other various woodland flora and fauna. Some of the trees you will encounter are old souls thought to date back to the 12th century. Other trees are mere youngsters by comparison and date back to the late 18th and early 19th centuries. An ancient avenue of horse chestnut trees fell foul of age and disease in more recent times and they are now being reintroduced to benefit bees and bats as well as other visitors and inhabitants of the woodland. There is also an active volunteer group who help with looking after this beautiful space, so you may spot them on your walk.

In the 14th century the woodland was a deer park and part of the Great Barr Estate which the Scott family developed. Along the route you will be taken to a marshy area that is crossed by planked bridges. This particular aspect has an eerie otherworldly sense to it and is a must for all earth fantasy novel readers as well as naturalists. It is simply stunning!

There is a children's play area at the Chapel Lane entrance to the site where you will find parking opposite St Margaret's Church.

This walk, though, is intended for the walker of any age to seek the tranquil nature of an ancient wood, and is an outing to be savoured and experienced slowly! The scents from the trees, their shapes and sheer size are magical as is the whole experience of walking under this great leafy canopy.

THE BASICS

Distance: 2 miles / 4km
Gradient: Light, with some steps
Severity: Easy
Time: 1 hr
Stiles: None
Map: OS Explorer 220 (Birmingham)
Path description: Variable: grass, gravel and earth
Start point: Lodge at entrance to Merrion's Wood. (GR SP 039960)
Parking: Car park at lodge off Skip Lane adjacent to A34 Birmingham Road (B43 7AN)
Toilets: None
Dogs: Allowed but site rules need to be adhered to
Refreshments: None

MERRION'S WOOD WALK

1. Access the wood to the left of the lodge via a gate and continue along the broad path into the woods. At a waymarker follow the yellow nature trail arrow, ignoring a small bridge that will lead further into the woods. Continue walking along the main path until you find a left turning at an information sign leading onto a tree bark path. We are now entering a dense area of woodland so keep  a look out for wildlife. Stay on the main path around this section of the walk and keep following the path as it bends around to the right. Follow the broad bark path to your left and keep left on this path until it reaches a narrow path with grass verges. Cross the three-planked bridge over a ditch and continue until path broadens out and becomes a tree barked pathway.

2. Turn left on the main gravel path that eventually leads to a broad grassed path taking you up towards a church. At the gate look left to Barr Beacon. Turn around here and retrace your steps along the path to re-enter the woods. Keep left on broad pebble path following signs for Beacon Way. Pass waymarker 2 and a little further along on the left is another waymarker, number 7. Ignore these markers and continue along the main broad path. A short distance from waymarker 7 is a left turning. Take this turning into a more densely covered area following the broad bark path round to the right. This is a marshy area so it may be wet and muddy after rain. Keep sight of the broad path on your right but stay on this narrower pathway for now.

3. At a T-junction there is a waymarker. Turn left here following the left-hand path through the trees and over a three-boarded bridge over a ditch followed by a two-boarded bridge over another ditch. Follow the path as it meanders towards waymarker 5. Continue straight ahead, crossing another three-boarded bridge that leads to a gate on main road. Turn around here and follow the path back to views of a 'pit' area. Walk back over the three-boarded bridge to waymarker 5 and then turn left. Keep marshland on the left. Descend a flight of boarded steps to a planked bridge over a pond. You may wish to spend some time here as this is a most tranquil section of the walk. Cross the bridge and follow the path to another bridge over a weir. Follow path left to a way marker. At a T-junction with a broad path, cross a two-boarded bridge and turn left onto the main path.

4. At a barred gate take in the view of the residential and urban surroundings this wood has. It is in stark contrast with the wood itself. At waymarker 6, turn around and walk back along the main path. Keep straight on up the hill. There will be woodlands to your right and an open green space to your left. Continue past a boarded bridge on the right and look for a small path on your left. Take this path to loop through the trees once more. At a wood-lap fence veer right, keeping on the designated path through the trees. Keep left on the main path as it goes through the wood and across a three-boarded bridge over a ditch to a junction. Where the wood opens out bear immediately right through the trees to join the main pebble path. Turn right onto the main path and continue to the lodge and car park.

© Morgan Bowers

© Morgan Bowers

© Roger Kidd

Baggeridge Country Park

BAGGERIDGE COUNTRY PARK

BAGGERIDGE COUNTRY PARK IS TO BE FOUND NOT FAR FROM SEDGLEY ON THE A463 AND IS FOUR MILES WEST OF DUDLEY. THE PARK IS OPEN DAILY THOUGH TIMES VARY DUE TO THE SEASON. THERE IS AMPLE CAR PARKING BUT THERE IS A CHARGE PER HOUR OR PER DAY. PLEASE CHECK THE INFORMATION BOARDS.

The park is accessed via a driveway that is clearly signposted from the A463 in Gospel End, which takes you over the more recently acquired Gospel End Common to the car park.

There are a wide range of events staged here and an adventure outdoor play area is also available, including aerial rope courses for those who are not faint-hearted! Other activities on site apart from walking include fishing and mountain biking, and there is also a miniature railway.

Although a very popular park you will find that within a few minutes' walk from the main car park and tea room/restaurant you will be transported into quietude. The transformed site, which once made up part of the Earl of Dudley's estate, of around 150 acres we see today was formerly opened by HRH Princess Anne 1983 and was formerly known as Baggeridge Colliery. It was neighbour to a brick works to which the chimney still stands testament today, and on this walk you will see some of the clay in the paths and roadways that served these works. In fact the whole area beneath your feet was criss-crossed with paths, roads and rails.

The colliery itself was opened in 1899 and was situated close to Gospel End Village. It was closed in 1968, the last Black Country Colliery to be shut down. This heralded a change in land usage from private pits to nationalised commercial mining to seeking other means of sources for local income. Mining had been recorded in the Black Country as far back as Roman times and probably preceded that period. To call this closure the end of an era would be nothing short of an understatement!

An area in the southern aspect of the park up to the Wishing Pools was part of Himley Hall, and was landscaped by none other than Capability Brown.

This walk has many features with its wetland flora and fauna and has such evocatively named places as White's Wood and White's Wood Pool. It is home to thousands of trees and a beautiful weir where cress was grown and farmed for the Dudley estate.

© Roger Kidd

THE BASICS

Distance: 3 miles / 5km
Gradient: Slight but with steep inclines and steps in places
Severity: Moderate walk
Time: 1½ hrs
Stiles: None
Map: OS Explorer 219 (Wolverhampton & Dudley)
Path description: Variable: tarmac, gravel and earth
Start point: Baggeridge Country Park car park. (GR SO 897930)
Parking: Car park at Baggeridge Country Park. (DY3 4HB)
Toilets: At visitor centre complex
Dogs: Allowed but site rules need to be adhered to
Refreshments: At cafe

BAGGERIDGE C.P. WALK

1. At the car park walk along the main path with the play area on the left. Turn left before a gravel path and walk through an overflow car park to a path bearing right and walk across another car park. Turn left signposted 'Bag Pool' and walk to the left of a red barrier gate, turning left at the next T-junction. Follow the main path. Walk under the railway bridge and at another T-junction turn left, walking towards the pool. At the next junction turn right, keeping the pool on your right, and cross a small planked bridge. At another junction turn right, keeping the pool on your right, and then turn left up the flight of steps marked 'Toposcope Trail'. Turn left up further steps and take time to look back before continuing to the top of hill and the viewpoint marker.

2. Walk left from the viewpoint, retracing your steps across the hill, and then turn left down the hill across the grass to enter a wooded area. Turn right at the bottom of the hill along a gravel path and then turn left over a grassed pathway with open meadowland. At a descent (be careful in wet weather), turn right and immediately left to a fork in the path and then turn right. Join the main path to enter White Wood; stay on the main path. Continue through a gate along the Miner's Path. Just before the gate to a housing estate turn right through an arch of trees to a green space and information board. Walk past the information board, staying on a gravel path, and walk over a small bridge crossing a ditch. There will be a walled section to your left.

3. Continue on the main path (muddy after rain) to a single-span brick railway bridge. Continue along the path and then turn left to a broad path and to a gate. Turn right at the gate, but don't go through it. At the pool follow a finger post to Himley Hall. Keep the pool on your right. On the left is an information board for the cress beds at a brick-built weir. The water rises here from a local spring. Cross a boarded bridge, keeping the pool on the right, and then turn right at a junction. Keep a flight of steps to your left with the pool overflow and descend some steps to the left of the weir. You will now see Island Pool. Follow the path to the right to a roofed information board. Himley Hall is accessible from here.

4. Turn around and retrace your steps back to Spring Pool and the cress beds and weir. Keep the pool to your left. Follow a broad path to a three-way junction. Take the middle path to a fingerpost marked 'car park'. Pass Lower Wishing Pool on your left and walk up a steep climb. Continue on the main path and cross a boarded bridge, bearing left along a partially tarmaced path. Pass 'Bob's Bench' on your right and keep following the path straight on, signposted 'car park'. Ascend the boarded steps. At a small path turn left towards the amphitheatre and then turn right. At the ridge turn left across the ridge towards trees. Here there are great views across the amphitheatre to your left. Turn right at the end and through a gate. At a fork take a minor left track with the adventure playground on your left. Turn left before the toilet blocks to walk around the sensory garden. Take time here to reflect and then take the slate path to your right to a gravelled area. Continue along a red gravel path to the car park start point.

THE DUDLEY Nº 1 CANAL

THE DUDLEY Nº 1 CANAL WAS BUILT IN 1792 PRIMARILY TO SERVE THE HUGE STEEL WORKS KNOWN AS ROUND OAK THAT EMPLOYED MANY LOCALS. THE SITE WAS BULLDOZED AFTER CLOSURE IN THE EARLY EIGHTIES TO SET UP THE DUDLEY ENTERPRISE ZONE, WHICH WAS LATER RENAMED THE MERRY HILL SHOPPING CENTRE.

There are two canal tunnels in this area, the first being the Dudley Tunnel which runs parallel to the Netherton Tunnel. The latter allows motorised boats; the former doesn't! If you choose to go through the Dudley Tunnel by boat then it's far more energetic! The canal route from the junction with the Stourbridge Canal at the bottom of the locks takes you through to Tipton, where you will pick up the rest of the canal in another walk in this book. There is no towpath through this tunnel, which passes through limestone caverns. Historically all boats would have to be 'legged', whereby the crew of the narrowboat would lie on their backs, feet against the tunnel wall and push one foot after the other!

The Delph Flight, where this walk begins, is known locally as The Nine Locks. The tenth lock is the pub, which will mark our start point and is situated on the Delph Road, Brierley Hill.

If you count the locks you will discover that there are actually only eight! This is due to a rebuild in 1858 following subsidence, but if you look around you will find remnants of the elusive ninth lock.

The walk will also take us to the Blower's Green Lock, which is the deepest single lock on the British Canal Network. This single lock replaced two earlier locks lost to subsidence. En route you will discover a beautiful viaduct and many old sections of bridges and walkways that transport you back to an earlier industrial time.

The canal was used mainly to ferry coal from the nearby coalfields known as 'nine-yard thick', which is said to be one of the contenders for naming the Black Country

'Black'. Other sections of canal where then built to ferry limestone from beneath Castle Hill in Dudley as part of the Earl of Dudley's industries.

Along the route you will also see the new 'Waterfront' and marina lined with hotels and bars as the leisure boat industries redefine the canal network. Looking down from the canalside vantage point you cannot miss the huge Merry Hill shopping complex.

THE BASICS

Distance: 5 miles / 9km
Gradient: Slight with steep lock flight
Severity: Easy walk
Time: 2½ hrs
Stiles: None
Map: OS Explorer 219 (Wolverhampton & Dudley)
Start point: The Tenth Lock pub. (GR SO 918863)
Path description: Variable: gravel and earth
Parking: On street near The Tenth Lock pub, on the B4172 Delph Road near Brierley Hill. (DY5 2TY)
Toilets: None
Dogs: Allowed but site rules need to be adhered to
Refreshments: None

THE DUDLEY Nº 1 CANAL WALK

1. The walk begins from the car park at The Tenth Lock pub. Turn right onto the canalside and follow the tarmac towpath. Ascend the eight locks. On the right is the old stables building where the towing horses could be stabled. The packets or passenger boats using the canals would have been given priority over trade boats in the early 19th century so the queues here would have been long and time-consuming during busy periods.

2. Walk over an iron rail bridge and as you cross the Delph Basin Bridge turn left under a road bridge and through the gate. Walk along Dudley Canal. This canal would link to the River Severn. Netherton Hill should be ahead of you in the distance with the church and Eave Hill Flats to the left. To the right is Rowley Hill, which was the highest grazing land in Britain. Be aware of mooring rings as potential trip hazards. To your right you will eventually see Merry Hill Shopping Centre. Walk under Greens Bridge towards the new waterfront. Walk under Level Street and the New Level Furnace Bridge passing Brewer's Wharf public house. Walk under Round Oak Bridge One and Round Oak Bridge Two and then under the Norish British Steel Bridge.

3. Walk under Woodside Road Bridge and then continue towards a junction and canal bridge. Cross the bridge and turn left. To your right is an old branch arm to the canal that is now filled in. Keep on the towpath.

4. Walk under Pear Tree Lane Bridge and cross the next bridge marked 1858 NBI Company. Turn right along the towpath once you have crossed the bridge. Go through a radar key gate up a path and walk under Dudley and Lye Waste Bridge to Park Head Lock, which is the deepest lock on the network, Blowers Green Pump House and lock. Continue to the higher level lock gates following the sign to Tipton Junction Old Line. Pass the lock-keeper's cottage on the left. Continue up towards another lock and further on to a viaduct. At Park Head Lock Bridge Number One take a left to Pensnett Basin Bridge, which was part of an old branch arm. Cross the Pensnett Bridge. There should be a green space ahead of you. Turn right and continue on the towpath to the entrance to the Dudley Tunnel.

5. Turn around and retrace your steps to Blower's Green Lock. Cross the lock gate at the pump house to pick up the towpath on your left. Walk under Blowers Green Bridge through a gate and along the narrow towpath keeping the canal on your left. This section is known as the Black Brook Canal. On your left is Netherton Hill again. Turn right under

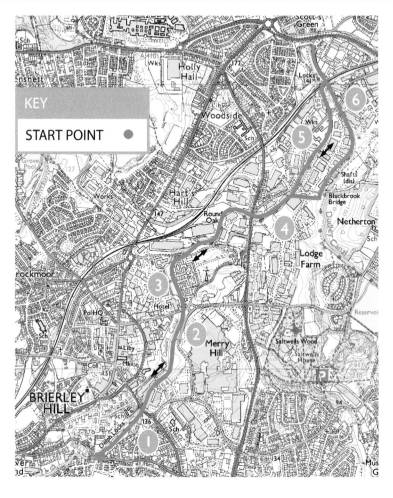

KEY

START POINT ●

a bridge at a profile-cut metal information board, then turn left and walk down a tarmac road to a main road following a blue cycle path signposted to Waterfront and Brierley Hill.

6. Walk up Black Brook Road to rejoin the canal, accessed through a small car park. Follow signage for Waterfront and walk under Pear Tree Lane Bridge and then across the canal at the next towpath bridge to retrace your steps back to the Tenth Lock pub. Walk back under Woodside Road and Norish Bridges. Continue under Round Oak Bridges Two and One, to the Waterfront and then to Lord Dudley, New Level Furnace and Green's bridges before walking under a blue girder-work bridge. At the top of the locks go through a radar key gate and under the Nine Locks Bridge. Cross the Delph Basin Bridge and descend the locks. The start point, the Tenth Lock, will be on your left.

GAS STREET BASIN

GAS STREET BASIN IS A THRIVING AREA OF REDEVELOPMENT
WITH ITS BARS AND RESTAURANTS AND ITS CLOSE PROXIMITY
TO THE INTERNATIONAL CONVENTION CENTRE (ICC),
NATIONAL INDOOR ARENA (NIA) AND OTHER PRESTIGIOUS
VENUES.

It is also linked to the Mailbox shopping centre where the BBC Studios are housed. Here you can see some of the displays, look through the windows on local radio and purchase on DVD the next must-have BBC series!

Gas Street Basin is situated in the City of Birmingham close to Chamberlain Square. It forms the junction of the Worcester and Birmingham Canal and the BCN (Birmingham Canal Navigations Company) mainline canal. The basin was built over the years from 1750 to 1799, the Birmingham section being completed in 1773. The Worcester and Birmingham Company started their build in Gas Street; however, the BCN wanted a physical barrier between the two canals to stop the new company benefiting from their water supply. This meant cargoes had to be manually transported from one boat to another across a barrier that was a mere 7 feet 3 inches across! In 1815 it was eventually agreed to place a bar lock and toll in place to allow passage from one canal to another. The Worcester bar is still in evidence and is used to moor boats, and is connected by a Horseley Bridge and Thomas Piggot Bridge manufactured in Horsley Heath, Great Bridge.

Birmingham was renowned for its lighter, white metal trades in silver and pewter before the car industries came along. However, the noisy neighbour Black Country would have relied upon these canal highways and motorways to transport its heavy goods far and wide. This walk will take you past Birmingham University and near to the site of the Chad Valley toy works to the chocolate capital Bournville, where tours of the factory are available should you wish. The village of Bournville is very picturesque and is testament to the patriarchal nature of the Cadbury family, offering decent housing, living and social conditions with a good helping of moral guidance!

The walk is a linear walk so that you can return along the canal to the city, making this a fairly long walk, or you can simply catch the train from Bourneville back to New Street station or hitch a bus ride back to Brum.

The canal towpaths are well maintained and there is plenty of opportunity to spot wildlife and flora and fauna as you leave the clutches of the city to join the greenery of the suburbs.

THE BASICS

Distance: 6 miles / 10km
Gradient: Slight
Severity: Moderate walk
Time: 2½ hrs
Stiles: None
Map: OS Explorer 220 (Birmingham)
Path description: Variable: tarmac, gravel and earth
Start point: Centenary Square, Birmingham. (GF SP 063868)
Parking: Local car parks in Birmingham and close to bus routes. (B1 2EP)
Toilets: At ICC and Mailbox
Dogs: Allowed but site rules need to be adhered to
Refreshments: At ICC complex, Mailbox and other outlets

GAS STREET BASIN WALK

1. The walk begins outside Birmingham Library and the Rep Theatre. Walk through the ICC building to the exit doors on Brindleyplace. There are bars and restaurants here. Walk across a blue brick bridge and turn immediately right off the bridge, down a flight of steps, and turn right onto the canal. Continue along the towpath under Broad Street bridge towards an ornate bridge known as Bar Lock where the two canals meet: the BCN and Worcester and Birmingham. Ahead is red brick building known as the Mailbox. The bridge ahead takes you towards the BBC  studio housed in the Mailbox. Continue on the towpath to the left of the bridge to continue to walk under the Salvage Turn bridge where you will find remnants of a rail track used to ferry goods around the basin. Suddenly modern development gives way to an older environment. Continue under Bridge 88, Granville Row, and pass a waymarker on your right.

2. At Bath Row walk under Bridge 87 along the brick towpath. Here you will see the canal and railway running parallel to each other. Continue under Bridge 86, Islington Row Middleway and the waymarker for the Vale. Over to your left is Edgbaston Hall, pool and golf club, and a little further on is, some would argue, the home of cricket, Edgbaston Cricket Ground. To your right are the Botanical Gardens and Chad Valley, where Chad Valley toys were made. The factory was started in the early 19th century by Anthony Bunn Johnson and was run by his son Alfred. The name comes from the nearby stream named Chad. The Botanical Gardens were opened in 1832 as an interest in plants grew after the 18th and 19th-century botanists introduced wide-ranging and varied species to the country from their excursions. Continue under Bridge 85, St James Road and on towards Edgbaston Tunnel, a twin-arch tunnel: canal beneath one arch and the railway under the other. Continue under a brick bridge, 84a. Continue towards bridges 84 and 83. You will see part of the Queen Elizabeth Hospital and Birmingham University railway station. Close to the hospital and on your right are the sites of Roman forts. Walk under University Road West Bridge and here you will see the railway swap to the other side of the canal before a footbridge and the Bristol Road bridge and Selly Oak railway station. A little beyond Selly Oak railway station you will see the railway switch back across the canal before Raddle Barn Road bridge. Here there are a number of properties that back onto the canalside, giving

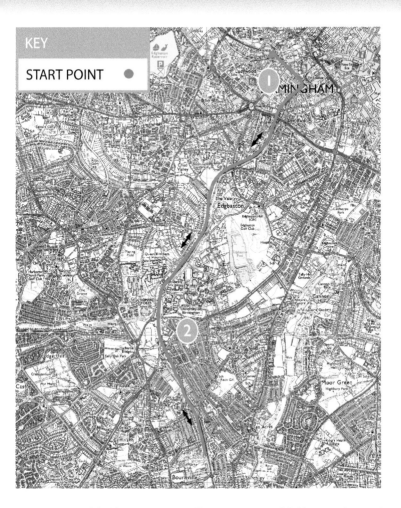

a continental feel in warm weather. There is also a small bridge over the canal which you will walk under. Take the ramp walk off to the right at Bournville Station, Bournville Lane, and turn right to go to the village. The colours of Cadbury's will suddenly become visible! The factory is a little walk away but a rewarding detour. The company started with John Cadbury in 1824 in a shop in Bull Street in the City of Birmingham. After experimenting with ingredients he expanded to his first factory, producing drinking chocolate, opened in 1831 in Crooked Lane and then moving to Bridge Street in 1847. By 1879 the next generation had expanded the business after a lean period of trade, taking over Bournbrook Hall and renaming the village Bournville. Walk back if you're feeling energetic! If not, catch the train back to Birmingham New Street.

BUMBLE HOLE

The walk starts at Windmill End, which is on the outskirts of Netherton and is accessed off the Dudley Road via Cole Lane, onto Vale Road and then Windmill End.

There is a small private car park on the left where permission has been granted to park cars at the time of publication. There is plenty of on-street parking but check with the volunteers at the visitor centre for peace of mind if using the car park!

The Bumble Hole site formed one of the backdrops to the children's television series Rosie and Jim as well as a Banks's beer advert!

The walk begins at the Bumble Hole nature reserve visitor centre on the towpath of the Dudley number 2 canal. The area was mined extensively in the 19th century to obtain coal from the thick seam that lay under the soil here. Because of the need to transport the coal and products from allied trades such as the steel industry along the canals, other industries set up on the canalside such as boat builders and maintenance yards.

The canal was built over a five-to-six-year period from 1793 to 1798 and connected with the Birmingham and Worcester canal at Selly Oak. Nearby you will see Cobb's Engine House, built in 1831, which housed a Watt beam engine to pump water from the deeply sunk mines. The blue brick bridge known as Cobb's Engine Bridge once carried trains across its back to ferry coal to fuel the engine in the pump house. Beyond this bridge lies the deep and dark Netherton Tunnel, which runs for the best part of two kilometres. It is dark, damp and very atmospheric if you are dressed for the occasion and equipped with torches! It is also rumoured to have some 'otherworldly presences' if you believe in that sort of thing! At the other end of the walk is Brewin's Tunnel.

With views to Sandwell, Wychbury Hill and lakes and pools, with industrial heritage and geological interests as well as wildlife including the enigmatic bat colonies, this walk is crammed with interest for all ages.

There is one steep climb, which can be omitted if necessary but if achievable affords some fantastic views of this post-industrial born-again leisure site. Don't forget there are toilets, snack foods and hot and cold drinks available at the visitor centre.

THE BASICS

Distance: 4 miles / 8km
Gradient: None
Severity: Easy
Time: 2 hrs
Stiles: None
OS Explorer 219 (Wolverhampton & Dudley)
Path description: Variable: tarmac, gravel and earth
Start point:
Parking: Car park at the Bumble Hole visitor centre. (DY2 9HU)
Toilets: At visitor centre
Dogs: Allowed but site rules need to be adhered to
Refreshments: At visitor centre

BUMBLE HOLE WALK

1. The walk begins at the car park by the former Dry Dock pub, now sadly closed. Walk back along a few yards and ascend a flight of planked steps to the towpath to the left of the old pub, now converted into flats. Turn right along the towpath towards Cobb's Engine House. At the towpath bridge to the right you will see a flight of steps. Do not cross the bridge. Ascend the steps towards the engine house. Follow a broad gravel path to the engine house. Continue past the engine house, keeping the building to your right. Walk up the hill following the grass path. At the top of the hill is a bench. To your right is Warren's Hall Nature Reserve, which marks part of the Sandwell/Dudley border. To your right is the Secret Pool and behind you there are excellent views of the reserve. Follow the higher path around the pool to a gated car park signed Warren's Hall. There will be another pool to your left and the 'Blow Cold Colliery' spoil heap

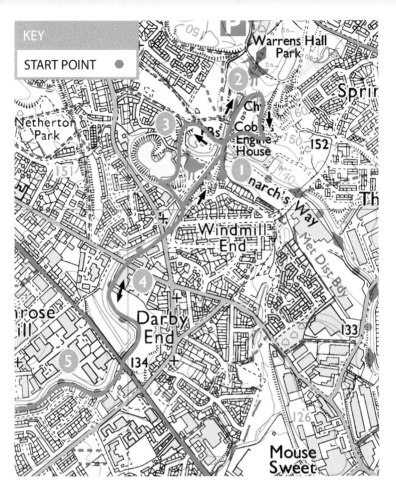

KEY

START POINT ●

Warrens Hall Park

Spri

Netherton Park

Ch

Cob

Engine House

152

narch's Way

Windmill End

Met Dist Bdy

Darby End

rose ill

134

133

126

Mouse Sweet

2. Keep the Secret Pool to your right and cross an overflow ditch for the pool. Take a narrow dirt path down the hill and head towards a bench in a grassed area keeping the engine house on your right. Looking out from this bench you will see Swan Pool. Turn 180 degrees and head for a bollarded bridge in front of you and cross the bridge to a broad tarmac path. To your right is Netherton Tunnel and to your left is the visitor centre.

3. Walk along broad gravel path to a T-junction and turn left. On your left is the Red Pool. Continue along and take a right fork past Bumble Hole on your right. Stay on the main gravel path. To your left take a cut through to the canal towpath. Cross Bumble Hole Bridge and turn right on the towpath and continue under the Fox and Goose Bridge. Stay on the towpath keeping the breaker's yard on your left at a bridge.

4. Stay on the towpath and walk between two blue brick gateposts to rejoin the canalside. Walk under Griffin Bridge. Pass Withymoor Island on your right and continue under Bishtons Bridge, remaining on the towpath passing a waymarker and a sign for Hingley's Stowable Anchor. The Netherton ironworks supplied the anchors for Titanic. Walk under Primrose Bridge, now known as Astle's Bridge after the legendary footballer Jeff Astle. Just along here is Lloyds Proving Centre, where chains were 'proved' for load bearing.

5. Cross a towpath bridge and continue along the main towpath and under Saltwells Bridge. To your left here you will see Lodge Farm Reservoir through the trees. Continue for another few yards to Brewins Tunnel and another kilometre to Blowers Green. Return along the towpath to Bumble Hole Bridge.

6. Cross the canal, turn right at a fork in the tarmac path leaving the towpath behind you and walk along the side of Bumble Hole, keeping it on your left. The footpaths here are tricky so keep right on the main path. At a railed section turn left to a viewing platform across the pool. Returning to a gravel path, turn left and then bear right on the main path to a T-junction and turn right towards the blue black bridge. Cross the bridge and turn immediately left after the bollards and descend a flight of steps to the towpath and turn right towards Netherton Tunnel. Walk a few yards into the tunnel to get an atmospheric feel of the canal! Then turn around and return on the towpath to the visitor centre and start point.

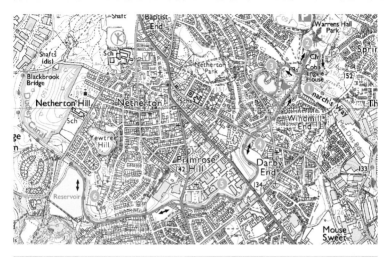

CANNOCK CHASE

THE NAME CANNOCK IS TAKEN FROM A CELTIC WORD
MEANING 'HIGH PLACE' AND IT IS SITUATED ON THE
SOUTHERN LIMITS OF STAFFORDSHIRE. ACCESS FOR
THIS WALK IS FROM THE VISITOR CENTRE CAR PARK ON
MARQUIS'S DRIVE, CANNOCK.

Cannock Chase is the last remaining section of a once great forest that became eroded as its wood and coal were exploited for industrial purposes. Originally timber was used for smelting iron, which subsequently gave way to the more efficient coal. At its height of mining there were over fifty coal mines in this coal-rich, small measure of land. With the last of the pits closing as recently as the early 1990s there is little evidence that remains of a once industrialised area.

The Chase contains Bronze Age burial grounds and was inhabited through the Saxon period through to the Norman kings, who turned the forest into a royal hunting ground used frequently up until the Stuart reign. With continued land usage and the near neighbour Black Country becoming a global manufacturing force in the late 18th and 19th centuries a 'ring road' of canals was formed to network its product.

Brindley Heath was farmed extensively by generations of Brindleys. In 1914 a hospital was built for returning soldiers and was further utilised beyond the Great War for miners. A church, club and school were built here to further serve the mining community in the 1920s. The railway line known as the 'Tackeroo Express' was built in 1915 to serve the fifteen hundred or so camp huts built on neighbouring heathland. The RAF then held a presence on the chase during the run-up to and throughout the second World War and the buildings were later decommissioned and demolished during the 1950s.

Cannock Chase has diverse wildlife, flora and fauna including fallow deer. Site management requests that for health and safety reasons all visitors should stay on the miles of well-defined paths that criss-cross the Chase. There is also a trail for partially sighted people, details of which can be found at the visitor centre. Cycling and horse riding are also encouraged along marked routes that are available at the centre. There is a café and shop as well as toilets. There are also many opportunities to sit and rest. If you are visiting in late summer the heather is in bloom and the smell is simply sublime!

THE BASICS

Distance: 3 miles / 5km

Gradient: Steep and slippery in places

Severity: Moderate walk

Time: 1¼ hrs

Stiles: None

Map: OS Explorer 244 (Cannock Chase & Chasewater)

Path description: Variable: tarmac, gravel and earth

Start point:

Parking: Pay and display car park at Cannock Chase visitor centre, Marquis's Drive (WS12 4PW)

Toilets: At visitor centre complex

Dogs: Allowed but site rules need to be adhered to

Refreshments: At visitor centre complex

CANNOCK CHASE WALK

1. Near to a bollarded section look to the right of a birch tree where there is a dirt path that leads to a blue and red marker numbered 23. Continue along a pebble path that takes you through the heather and at a fork in the path take the right fork towards the road. This is Brindley Heath Road. Cross the road carefully and look for a blue marker directly opposite. Continue along this path into the trees. It can be muddy here. Follow the main forest floor path.

2. Pass blue markers 22 and 21 and at a T-junction at marker 20 turn right along the former route of the Tackeroo Railway, which once served the buildings on site. There is evidence of 'klinker' or iron slag along here from iron smelting and furnace industries. There is a heather embankment one side and grassland to your left. On your right is a viewing

platform should you wish to climb the steps. Here you will get a bird's eye view of the landscape that unfolds before you. Continue along the main path, passing marker 7a. Ignore a bridge crossing on your right. At this point take time to look at the pools on your right: a very reflective and thought-provoking place.

3. At marker 7 there is a crossroads. Turn right along the pebble path and then continue past the First World War filter beds on your left, continuing up to the top of the hill where you'll see the concrete rafts of demolished buildings. The area just beyond here is known as the flint fields due to its geology. Flint tools have been found left lying around, which is evidence of early settlements. Before reaching the road turn around and retrace your steps back towards the crossroads at the bottom of the hill.

4. At the crossroads turn right at blue marker 7. We are now heading towards the car park at Brindley Bottom. Pass waymarker 8 and enter the car park through a rustic gated section, then look dead ahead to another blue marker, number 9. Continue up and left along the pebble-based path into the woods. This section is quite steep. Pass marker 10, where the path bends right, and continue on to waymarker 11, and carry on following the main route to waymarker 12 where you will turn left onto a dirt path.

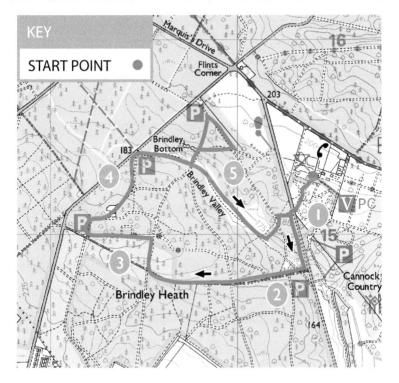

5. There are many well-defined paths through the woods at this point which you can choose to add on and explore if you wish, but please remember to rejoin this path! For this walk continue to waymarkers 13 and 14. At this point you will see the remains of the First World War hospital on your left. At marker 15 turn right to marker 16, where there are extensive views of the heathland, especially beautiful in early September. Continue downhill to waymarker 17 and turn left along Duffields Lane to waymarker 18. Continue along the main track to Duffields Road car park. At marker 19 turn left and on to a crossroads, then turn right at blue marker 20. The path is steep here but the views are stunning. Turn right at marker 21 and continue on the main path through the trees towards Brindley Heath Road. At marker 22 cross the road carefully and rejoin the path opposite. Walk along the path to marker 23 and then continue on to the car park entrance opposite the visitor centre. This concludes the walk.

GALTON VALLEY

GALTON VALLEY IS SITUATED OFF BRASSHOUSE LANE IN THE TOWN OF SMETHWICK. THERE IS A CAR PARK IN THE LANE OPPOSITE A SCHOOL AND ADJACENT TO WEST BROMWICH ALBION'S FOOTBALL FOUNDATION.

On arriving at this town you will immediately see the meeting point of canal, rail and road and its geographical importance. On the outskirts of the town from atop a pedestrian-bridged walkway there is the opportunity to see this complex interchange to its full extent.

Located on the edge of multicultural Smethwick, Galton Valley harks back to the industrial dawn of the late 18th century when great minds and invention began to shape the modern world with transport infrastructure and technology. James Brindley and Thomas Telford defined the landscape with canals, bridges and tunnels whilst Watt, Newcomen and Boulton drove industry forward with their methods of engineering. Examples of all are represented here either physically or in spirit, the landmark building being the pumping station that drew water to the top of the lock system.

This walk will take you along the higher level of canal that Brindley tried to send over a hill, and then back along the low-level canal that Telford created by channelling through it! We will see some of the oldest remaining locks in the country and discover how technology both tamed and harnessed natural geological features to their full practical extent.

The walk will take us underneath the M5 motorway close to one of the busiest junctions in Europe. It will take us to some of the quietest natural beauty spots in the region and on to areas of noisy industry and peaceful solitude. What a heady mix! There are fine examples of bridges and aqueducts so industrial archaeologists should really enjoy this walk.

Part of this route will take us on the Soho Loop, which is a short offshoot of the main canal that skirts the area of Soho. This town was where the Lunar Society used to meet. Amongst the luminaries were Boulton, Brindley and Watt.

The informal group called themselves 'The Lunarticks' and were basically a luncheon club for great minds to meet from the fields of art and science. In fact one of the members was Samuel Galton, whose name is given to bridge and valley here, while others included printer John Baskerville of typeface fame and the potter Josiah Wedgwood. Their regular meeting place was Soho House, with meetings being always held on a full moon.

THE BASICS

Distance: 8 miles / 13km

Gradient: None

Severity: Moderate walk

Time: 3 hrs

Stiles: None

Map: OS Explorer 220 (Birmingham)

Path description: Variable: tarmac, gravel and earth

Start point: Brasshouse Lane, Smethwick. (GR SP 019889)

Parking: Car park in Brasshouse Lane. (B67 7QY)

Toilets: None

Dogs: Allowed but site rules need to be adhered to

Refreshments: None

GALTON VALLEY WALK

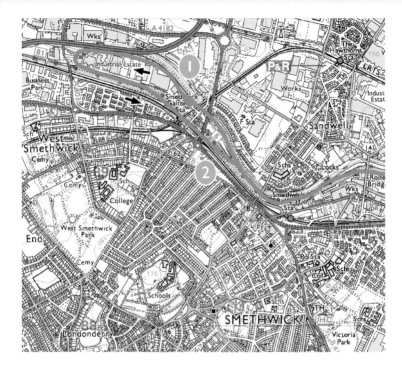

1. The walk begins at the pump house, which is accessed by crossing the road bridge just past the West Bromwich Albion Federation building and descending down the steps to the towpath. Walk along the same side of the towpath as the pump house, keeping the pump house on your left towards Wolverhampton. Continue along the high level canal to Summit Tunnel.

2. Once you have emerged from beneath the motorway look for Lath Lane on your left before reaching Spon Lane. At the main road turn left towards a blue brick bridge. Turn left down the steps to join the lower level canal and walk back towards Birmingham. Walk under Spon Lane Bridge and continue through Galton Tunnel and the pump house stack should now be visible on your left. You can return to the start point here if you choose the steps to you left. If not continue on gravel towpath on lower level under Brasshouse Lane Bridge. On your left there is a man-made weir draining water from the high level. Walk under the Engine Arm Bridge. Walk under Rolfe Street Bridge and up a blue brick path up Towing Path Bridge to Smethwick Junction. If you turn left here you can return along the high level canal to Galton Valley.

3. To continue turn right along the towpath towards Birmingham, walking under a Horseley ironworks bridge. Continue under Rabone Road Bridge. Walk under a railway bridge

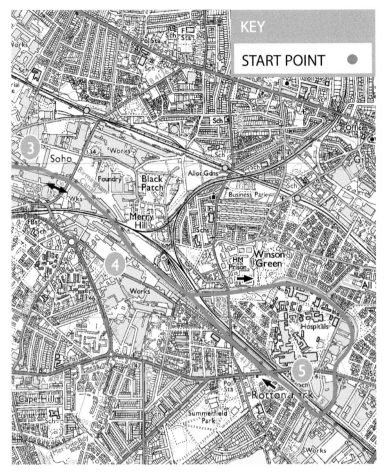

KEY

START POINT ●

following the towpath over a bridge section and interchange. Stay on the towpath to Birmingham, continuing under another Horseley Bridge dated 1848.

4. At the Metro stop turn left along the canal signposted Soho Loop. At this point you can turn around and follow the towpath all the way back to Galton Valley on the high-level canal. To continue to Soho walk under the Winson Green Railway Bridge and follow the towpath as it gradually bends to the right over approximately the next mile and a half (2 km). Walk over a roving bridge to stay on the main towpath to Winson Green Junction. Pass a canalside marker to Rotton Row and walk under Asylum Bridge. Soho will be to your left and ahead is the telecommunications tower in Birmingham. Walk past the moorings at the Soho Branch and continue over the roving bridge to rejoin the towpath. On your left is the Birmingham skyline with the canal on your right. Continue under

GALTON VALLEY WALK

Springhill Bridge and past factories which form the canal wall. Cross a steep ramp and over a roving bridge to continue along the towpath to Railway Bridge Road and then onto Rotton Park Junction. Follow the path to the left over a bridge. Follow signpost to Wolverhampton. Walk under Lee Bridge 1826 and Winson Green Bridge to Smethwick Junction. At the turnaround Bridge 3 look for the rope grooves. At Smethwick Junction walk under the bridge and immediately cross the second bridge named Smethwick Towing Path Bridge. Turn immediately right at the towpath junction once you have crossed the bridge to remain on the higher level canal.

5. Continue to Galton Valley under Pope's Bridge past the locks marked 3 and 2. Walk past Sandwell Locks Bridge where you see the lock-keeper's house. On your left is a footbridge and aqueduct that once served industrial units. Walk up and over a roving bridge to continue on towpath. On your left in a few yards is the man-made weir that you passed on the lower level. The pump house now becomes visible where the walk will end at Brasshouse Lane Bridge. Take steps up to the road level and return to the car park.

ABOUT THE AUTHOR

Brendan Hawthorne was born in Tipton on 12 March 1961. He has lived and worked in the Black Country all of his life and is a great believer in keeping the oral traditions of language and anecdotes alive in an ever-changing world of technology.

After leaving school, with no fixed education, he went to work in a factory as an electrician on heavy goods vehicles, which is where he believes his education truly began!

Since leaving industry in 1996 he has worked in several professional roles and is now a freelance writer, songwriter and performance poet, achieving Poet Laureate of Wednesbury status in 2014.

Much of his performance work echoes the humour and hardships of a region whose scars are still healing in this post-industrial age.